Jesus in Our Midst

Chiara Lubich

Jesus in Our Midst

Source of Joy and Light

Edited by
Donato Falmi and Judith Povilus

New City Press

Hyde Park, New York

Published in the United States by New City Press
202 Comforter Blvd., Hyde Park, NY 12538
www.newcitypress.com
©2019 New City Press (English Translation)

Cover design by Leandro De Leon
Layout by Miguel Tejerina

Originally published in Italian as *Gesú In Mezzo*
Copyright 2019 by Citta' Nuova Editrice, Rome, Italy.

Library of Congress Control Number: 2019951059

ISBN 978-1-56548-704-4 (paperback)
ISBN 978-1-56548-704-9 (e-book)

Printed in the United States of America

Contents

Series Preface[1]

"To those who follow you, leave only the gospel."

Chiara Lubich has articulated the gospel in many ways, which are outlined in twelve cornerstones: *God-love*, the *will of God*, the *Word of God*, *love of neighbor*, the *new commandment*, the *Eucharist*, the gift of *unity*, *Jesus crucified and forsaken*, *Mary*, the *Church-communion*, the *Holy Spirit*, *Jesus present among us*.

Since they emerged in the late 1940s, these points have been inscribed in the souls and in the lives of thousands of people from every corner of the earth. Nevertheless, since Chiara Lubich's death in 2008, what has been missing is a document that combined many texts, including those yet unpublished, that would illustrate them. This series of books seeks to deepen our understanding of these twelve cornerstones by presenting three sources from which they have emerged:

- the dimension of her personal testimony, especially as Chiara Lubich understood, deepened and lived these points;

- the theological dimension of reflecting on the mystery of God and of humankind;

- the dimension of incarnating these points in human life via a communitarian experience, in line with Vatican II (see Lumen Gentium 9).

---

1. This volume contains Chiara Lubich's thought and experience on "Jesus in Our Midst." While it is the twelfth in this series of titles originally published in Italian by Città Nuova, it is the sixth to be translated in its complete form and published by New City Press

The series will include as many as twelve books, through which it is hoped that readers may discover:

- A great spiritual teacher who can accompany them in their spiritual life;

- A deeper appreciation of the communal aspect of Christian life, and the implications of a communitarian spirituality for the Church and humanity;

- A deeper and more personal understanding of Chiara Lubich's life and thought that they can apply in their everyday life.

Introduction

In a world where social communication networks are multiplying out of all proportion, paradoxically there seems to be an ever-increasing sense of isolation and loneliness. In this context, one wonders about the deeper meaning of life. How are we fulfilled? Where do we find true happiness? On the one hand, society exalts individualism and self-determination. But on the other, many people yearn for authentic and profound relationships. They ask, often with a sense of anxiety, "What is the meaning of my life? How can I reconcile seemingly conflicting demands? How do we build relationships of true communion?" By living the experience of Jesus in the midst, as presented in this book, we can find the answer to these questions that touch the heart of every person, an answer that does not come from human reasoning, but from life.

When Chiara Lubich met Bishop Giovanni Battista Montini, the future Pope Paul VI, at the Vatican in 1953, she spoke to him about the life of the newly born Focolare Movement. She told him that they had discovered something more valuable than all the treasures of the world, including the works of art in the Vatican, worth more than the beauty of nature, worth even more than one's family ties. This treasure was the presence of the living Christ wherever two people, even those who are young or are repentant sinners, are united in his name, ready to love one another to the point of giving their lives for one another. Strong words, one might say, for a young woman speaking to a clergyman who was in a position of great authority in Rome. However, her strong conviction came from having lived this experience with others and making it the central point of the new life they had undertaken together. It was a reality for them and they called it very simply, "Jesus in the midst."

They had been living in this way for several years and had already discovered that their life took a qualitative leap for the better when love for Christ circulated among them. They experienced peace that is "not of this world" (see Jn 14:27), new ardor, the ability to penetrate the Scriptures and understand the steps they had to take. All these fruits could be explained by the promise of Jesus: "Where two or three are gathered in my name, I am there among them" (Mt 18:20). Complementing this passage, and standing as the basis for it to be fulfilled, was the New Commandment: "Just as I have loved you, you also should love one another" (Jn 13:34).

Today, in the Catholic Church, the idea that Christ is present in the community has become a familiar concept, but in the ecclesial environment before the Second Vatican Council, when the juridical and institutional structure of the Church was more evident and emphasis was placed, above all, on sacramental practice, this experience was almost unknown. It is emblematic that the final sentence of a 1960 dossier of the Italian Episcopal Conference concerning "the Focolare phenomenon," criticizes the concept "Jesus in the midst" as "an unknown doctrine."[2] Later, through her various ecumenical contacts, Chiara discovered that the living presence of Christ in the community was a theme dear

2. See Bennie Callebaut, *The Birth of the Focolare. History and sociology of a charism 1943-1965* (Rome: Città Nuova, 2017), 401-402.

to Christians of the Reformed Churches, one of their fundamental premises, albeit with different nuances.

But what was it for Chiara and the small group around her? Certainly not only a concept or a doctrine, but—as we can see from her words to Bishop Montini—the very real presence of the risen Christ "where two or three are gathered in his name." Therefore, he is present not only upon the altar in the Eucharist, but in families, on the streets of the city, in places of work, in schools . . . He was "God close to us," present in the community of those who loved one another as he loved us. This understanding gradually emerged in the documents of the Catholic Church as well, which for some centuries after the Council of Trent had spoken of a "real" presence almost exclusively with reference to the Eucharist. Then, with the encyclical *Mystici Corporis Christi* ("On the Mystical Body of Christ") issued in 1943 by Pope Pius XII, the Church was presented as the Mystical Body of Christ. Since then the horizons have been opened wide; in 1965 the title was explicitly recognized by Pope Paul VI in *Mysterium Fidei* ("The Mystery of Faith"). This encyclical outlines the various equally "real" ways in which Christ is present in the Church: in the Word, in the sacraments, and in the assembly of Christians united. The time had come for the Church to be seen as "communion." The words of Matthew 18:20 are found in almost every document produced by the Second Vatican Council. Therefore, the experience that Chiara shared with Bishop Montini foreshadowed this new perspective developing within the Catholic Church.

The reality and practice of "Jesus in the midst," which came into evidence in a special way with the charism of unity, is nothing more, as Chiara often said, than the life of the Church put into practice. It is the life of the Church seen as the Mystical Body of Christ (see 1 Cor 12:12-27), in which love circulates in the communion among its members. In the Church so understood, what is already potentially present—Jesus present among us—is implemented, like a dimmable lightbulb whose intensity can be raised from minimum to maximum, or, to use another of Chiara's images, like a network of dark tunnels that are lit up with love. It is the "already and not yet" of the eschatological perspective. Through baptism, we are inserted into the risen Christ, and with Jesus in our midst, we become what we already are.

It is useful to examine the relationship in Chiara Lubich's thought between the concepts of unity (see Jn 17:21) and Jesus in the midst. Sometimes she equates them and, at other times, she says that one is a prerequisite for the other. She describes them from two perspectives: the ascetic (what is required of us) and the mystical (the gift of God). In the mystical sense unity is a gift from God that transforms us into the risen Christ, individually and all together, in a single movement of love. Many of Chiara's texts link unity to the mystery of the Eucharist. We can and ought to prepare ourselves to accept the gift by creating the necessary "space." We do that by living mutual love unconditionally (see Jn 15:12-13). However, this divine gift transcends our human nature; it is always a gift from above. On the one hand, it has already been given to us, once and for all, in the paschal mystery of Christ; on the other, its full manifestation in our relationships remains incomplete. Chiara therefore speaks of Jesus in the midst as a particular grace, the grace that comes when unity is accomplished, when the "light is switched on" and Christ is manifested among us.

12

Another key point that has a strong connection both with Jesus in the midst and with unity is *Jesus forsaken*. This expression refers to the cry of Jesus on the cross: "My God, my God, why have you forsaken me?" (see Mt 27:46; Mk 15:34) and the believer's adherence to him forsaken and risen, embraced in every suffering or limitation. Jesus forsaken teaches how to not turn in on ourselves, but rather to project outwards in love for others, having an attitude that involves the death of oneself, the crucifixion of one's ego. It is an act of free and deliberate self-denial, almost cancelling out oneself, and yet it is inspired by love, and so not negative or destructive. "This total renunciation is important," Chiara said, "and it is necessary also to renounce even our inspirations, even what might be divine in us, like Jesus forsaken did, in order to reach unity, in order to have Jesus in our midst." Jesus forsaken therefore expresses the radical nature of the love required of Christians to achieve unity, loving one another *as* Jesus loved us. However, we need to emphasize that it is all based on love and is followed by the resurrection.

Collecting the texts contained in this book posed a double challenge. First of all, we had an abundance of sources to choose from—thousands of documents, including formal and informal presentations, personal writings, official addresses, and answers to questions from members of the Movement. These texts all illustrate the meaning and centrality of Jesus in the midst for the Work of Mary[3] and for the Church. Secondly, there also are texts and talks that carefully describe concrete practices that developed over many

---

3. "Work of Mary" is the official name of the Focolare Movement under which it was approved by the Roman Catholic Church in 1962.

years on how to ensure and maintain such a presence in various kinds of relationships.

Chiara realized that she had received a charism not for herself or for a small group, but for the good of many, and could not keep it for herself. She had the burning desire to communicate it: "I will speak and write, I will communicate everything through any means," she wrote in 1949, and for more than 60 years this is what she did. Therefore, reducing all of this to a small book was daunting. Some of the most meaningful and important texts about Jesus in the midst have already been published in the previous volumes of this series. Each year since 2011, one of the twelve points of the spirituality, as listed in the Statutes, has been offered to members of the Movement to live during that year. Therefore, books with excerpts of Chiara's writing have been published on God-love, the will of God, the Word, love of neighbor, the New Commandment, the Eucharist, unity, Jesus forsaken, Mary, the Church, and the Holy Spirit. Now we are considering Jesus in the midst, but having reached this last point, it seems that Jesus in the midst had already been covered within almost all the other points.

This should not really come as a surprise, since Jesus in the midst has to permeate the whole life of the members of the Work of Mary which, as stated in its Statutes, aims at being a presence of Mary, almost a continuation of her, generating Christ spiritually in the world wherever two or three are present. "Everything that is done is valid only if he is present," Chiara said, "otherwise nothing has any meaning." And in her diary she wrote: "The various points of our spirituality actually explain Jesus in the midst" in the sense that they "open up its various aspects, like opening out a fan" (see Diary, April 13, 1967).

Therefore, throughout the chapters of this book, we will see at times this fan opened out, with frequent references to the other points of the spirituality we have already discussed in the past. Specifically, we note:

- When considering the discovery of Jesus in the midst during the early days of the Movement, what comes to the fore are love for one's neighbor and in particular, mutual love, which brings about his presence among us.

- In the second chapter, we look at the effects of the presence of the risen Lord among people living in unity. It becomes evident that he enlightens our minds to understand the will of God and penetrate into the meaning of Scripture.

- In the third chapter, in considering the praxis, that is, how to obtain and maintain the presence of Jesus in the midst, we discover that it is intrinsically linked to the life of unity and the love for Jesus forsaken.

- In looking at the relationship between Jesus in the midst and the Work of Mary, we see, among other things, that just as Mary gave Jesus to the world, her Work has the goal of giving Christ to the world, spiritually present among "two or more."

- The chapter on Jesus in the midst and the Church presents the ecclesial dimension of his presence where two or three are gathered in his name, which is crucial for ecumenism. We also see the emergence of the relationship between Jesus in the midst and the Holy Spirit.

- In the last chapter, in which we consider how Jesus in the midst renews every aspect of life in society, the theme of unity comes up again, but now in its universal dimension: "That they may all be one" (Jn 17:21).

It is interesting to note that in the latest revision of the Statutes of the Work of Mary[4] (2007), where the twelve points of the spirituality are listed, Chiara moved Jesus in the midst to the last place, explaining that he is, yes, the point of departure and an ever present reality, but he is also "in a special way, the point of arrival" of our spirituality. By following the formation God used with the first focolarini at the beginning of the Movement, we too begin by believing in God's love, by doing his will, and by loving one another. Then we discover that the profound unity in Christ that we achieve can be called by his name—Jesus in our midst—and that this particular presence of his has to be taken everywhere. This way of life requires holiness of us, but at the same time leads us to holiness. It is not, however, the holiness of an individual, but of *the* Saint, of Jesus himself in the midst of any two people, even repentant sinners, who are united in his name. He is *the* Saint for our times, as Chiara often used to say, the one the world is waiting for. "Jesus among us as the premise or principle, as the means for our becoming holy and as the end."[5]

In 1948, Igino Giordani, editor of the magazine *Fides*, published an article by Chiara in which she

---

4. The Focolare Movement was approved by the Catholic Church in Rome in 1962, under the official name, "Work of Mary," which indicates the Movement as a whole with all its branches, vocations, and movements.

5. From an unpublished text written in 1950.

wrote passionately about Jesus in the midst, words that seem prophetic for our times. Seeing and praising the fruits of unity in the community of the Movement around her, in the families, in the businesses, and in the schools, Chiara foresaw the "beginning of a new era, the era of Jesus," and she continued, "all this is because the only principle, the only means, the only end is Jesus. Jesus in us. Jesus among us. Jesus, the aim of time and of eternity.

"People are agonizing over the need to find solutions to the critical issues of our time, but they will only find them in Jesus, and not only in Jesus living in the depths of each individual heart, but in Jesus reigning *among* people.

"They won't need time to discuss things because Jesus will very clearly show them, if they are and remain united with others in his name, what has to be done to restore true peace to the world."[6]

Please note

Texts in this volume from published sources are cited. Unpublished texts are not. Transcripts of unpublished audio recordings have been edited for clarity.

---

6. See Chiara Lubich in *Fides*, October 1948: 279-280.

Chapter I

Jesus in the Midst, Fruit of Mutual Love

The Discovery and Life of Jesus in the Midst During the "Early Days"

Towards the end of 1944, due to wartime circumstances in Trent, Chiara and some of her first companions began sharing a small apartment in Piazza Cappuccini. They had no idea of what was about to come to life. They simply understood that the Gospel had to be taken seriously, that its words were not only to be meditated on, but to be put into practice. Among these were all the passages about love for neighbor and love for one another, including Jesus' New Commandment. It was a strategy God used to lead them to a new discovery, that of the presence of Jesus among those who love one another, which soon became the cornerstone of their existence.

1. Where There is Love, There is God

Jesus in the midst is the fruit of the mutual love Jesus asked of his disciples, who had to be ready to give their lives for one another (see Jn 13:34), that is, "to be consumed in unity." Already in the very first years of this new "adventure," in trying to live like this, Chiara and her first companions experienced what she described as "a qualitative leap" in their spiritual life. They noticed that they had new peace and light, supernatural joy previously unknown, and fruits that were disproportionate to their human efforts, such as unexpected conversions. They experienced—as some writings later testify—the presence of God within the community, which they soon connected with the presence of Jesus, who promised to be present with "two or three gathered in his name."

The first text in this section dates to 1950, a few years after the "discovery" of Jesus in the midst. We find here clearly expressed all the fundamental elements of his presence: it is an unmistakably real presence, it is linked to mutual love and unity, and it has tangible effects.

A delectable mystery

From "A Little Harmless Manifesto"
Trent, 1950

We did not take a single step if we were not all united by mutual love: "above all" (see 1 Pt 4:8) . . . The strength that came to us from unity, brought about by mutual love, soon led us to reflect on the sentence of Jesus: "Where two or three are gathered in my name, I am there among them" (Mt 18:20). We saw the wonderful effects brought about by this unity, especially through our prayers, since he had said: "Truly I tell you, if two of you agree on earth about anything you ask, it will be done for you by my Father in heaven" (Mt 18:19).

Therefore, Jesus was among us because we were united in his name. This delectable mystery compelled us to keep our unity strong, so as to always have him among us.

And his presence was felt above all in an abundance of light, love and strength, just as his absence was felt when for a few moments we were not living in unity, because one or another of us had not done the will of God. That was when everything seemed to fall apart. The light was extinguished, the light that came from him and that made us see his words as so beautiful, so revolutionary, so full of life and so necessary in order to be true Christians. What had previously been so clear because we had *seen* and loved, now had to be *believed* in the darkness of faith. Doing any good deeds was heavy and almost impossible. Everything seemed empty and useless, until through mutual love (with the return of the brother or sister who had erred by not loving), unity was re-established and Jesus returned among us, to shine in our souls like the sun, spreading charity and peace, which made us powerful and capable of every sacrifice. Alone we wouldn't be able to carry on.

Unity became our passion, because with unity Jesus came among us. Therefore, unity with God by carrying out his whole will for us. Unity with our brothers and sisters as the fulfilment of the New Commandment of Jesus, as an expression of our love for the Father. Unity with Jesus because Jesus in the midst meant Jesus in us made *one* by him through our mutual love, sharing in his light, his strength, and his love. He has said: "the glory that you have given me I have given them" (Jn 17:22). Therefore united among us.

Before, we had mingled together as brothers and sisters. Now Jesus in the midst was like the fire that melts two metals into a third element, which has qualities different from the other two. Likewise, we noticed that two people united in the name of Jesus, who loved each other with the love with which Jesus had loved them, lost their natural human qualities in this "fusion" and acquired the divine qualities that made them one, while at the same time keeping them distinct, each with a very unique supernatural[7] personality. They became another Jesus.[8]

The prelude of a communitarian spirituality

Let's go back a little bit in time. Before the birth of the first focolare household[9] and the first written reference to Jesus in the midst, God prepared Chiara for what was to become—together with Jesus forsaken—one of the fundamental cornerstones of the spirituality of the future Movement. In November 2003, during an ecumenical conference of bishops in Rocca di Papa, she recalled an inspiration she had had in Loreto, Italy, in 1939, which she later related to Jesus in the midst.

*From a talk to the bishop-friends
of the Focolare Movement*
Rocca di Papa, November 26, 2003

Jesus in the midst of his people. When did the idea of Jesus in our midst, the highest expression of the spirituality of unity, first appear in our Movement? Four

---

7. The word "supernatural" is used in theology to express a quality of divine grace that lifts a believer to a share in the life of God, beyond a merely "human" way of being.

8. See Chiara Lubich, *Manifesto* (London: New City, 1975), 24-6.

9. The term "focolare" (Italian for "hearth" or "fireside") refers to a small community of either men or women who have consecrated their lives to God as single or married persons and who take the commitment to live in unity with one another. They are referred to as focolarine (women) or focolarini (men).

years before the date that marks the birth of the Movement, in 1939, when I was 19 years old, I was invited to Loreto for a conference for Catholic youth.

Although I was following the course, I felt strongly attracted to go into the church, which, like a fortress, seemed to safeguard the "little house"—as we have always called it—where the holy family of Nazareth is thought to have lived.

I went back there several times during the course, and each time I knelt down next to those walls blackened by the lanterns, something new and divine enveloped me, moving me deeply and almost crushing me. I imagined and contemplated the virginal life of Mary and Joseph with Jesus in their midst.

I did not understand the reason for that strong impression. Later, over the years, everything became clear to me. It was the call to a life of communion among persons who live with "Jesus in their midst."

That was the prelude to a spirituality that is not only individual, but also communitarian, the "spirituality of unity," which all those who would become part of the newborn Movement would be called to live.

From the prelude to the implementation

This vague intuition, a mere foreshadowing of what would come, began to take shape in a very natural way when the first group of focolarine began to live together in Trent, in a small apartment on Piazza Cappuccini. Gradually they came to understand what would later be considered the main points of the spirituality: God-Love, the will of God, mutual love, the New Commandment, unity, Jesus forsaken, etc. As the following note shows, Chiara herself, in reading something in a book many years later, understood more clearly how the Holy Spirit had gradually instructed her in a way of life that then led to having Jesus present in their midst.

From a written note
October 20, 2000

Whereas in Loreto I had the vague idea of a family and of Jesus present within it, I certainly did not know *how* to have Jesus really present among us.

Last night, when I woke up, I had the clear impression that I had received a revelation back then (that's how I saw it), when, as the points of the spirituality gradually opened up for us, I came to understand *how* to have Jesus among us. I saw him as our principal characteristic, and the requirements to have him present were revealed to us one by one. These were the various points of the spirituality. Therefore, we, and perhaps only we, have this possibility. Are we going to disregard it? Shouldn't we value having Jesus in our midst as an absolute necessity?

2. He Revealed Himself

In the early years of the Movement, although she didn't yet use the term "Jesus in the midst" and made no explicit reference to Matthew 18:20, Chiara spoke expressly of the presence of Christ as the result of the unity between two or more people. Thus, for example, in the notes prepared for a meeting with the young people of the Franciscan Third Order in 1946, which was entitled "Unity," she wrote:

"When unity passes, it leaves only one trace: Christ."[10] *"Quietly," Chiara later commented, "like an invisible brother, he had joined our group."*

Then, at a given point—the exact date is not documented—reading in Matthew's Gospel, "Where two or three are gathered in my name, I am there among them" (Mt 18:20), Chiara understood that these words explained the profound reality she had been experiencing for some time with her first companions. It was the presence of Jesus himself among them, as he had promised. Therefore, first they had had an existential experience, which was later followed by the understanding of the deeper reality. Chiara attributed this illumination to the presence of Jesus in their midst, which they were already living without fully understanding it.

From an answer to a question from the focolarini at the school of formation
Loppiano,[11] May 20, 1969

Chiara, when did you first discover Jesus in the midst?

It was one of the first ideas that came to us. I discovered him because he was there. In the sense that . . . by loving one another, we had fulfilled the requirements for him to be present among us. He enlightened us; he made us understand the Gospel. That's when we understood the meaning of the phrase, "Where two or three are gathered in my name, I am there among

---

10. Donato Falmi and Florence Gillet, eds., *Unity* (New York: New City Press, 2015), 49.

11. Loppiano is the first of the Focolare's little towns set up by the Movement as examples of small settlements where the rule of life is mutual love. Loppiano, in Tuscany near Florence, started as a formation center for those who aspired to live in Focolare communities anywhere in the world.

them." He is the one who revealed himself; we didn't discover him. We understood that he was in our midst when we were united in his name, because when he was there, we felt joy . . . everything had meaning, the number of people following us grew and multiplied. It was evident—it was a revolution!

Mary knows that Jesus is present where two or more are united

In the two letters that follow, both of the same date, we find perhaps the first time Chiara referred to this passage in Matthew's Gospel: "Where two or three are gathered in my name, I am there among them" (Mt 18:20). She was speaking about being united as one through mutual love.[12] It is significant that Mary is mentioned in both letters in reference to this presence of Jesus. As Chiara would later state, Mary wanted to give life to a movement of people through whom her Son would live spiritually again on earth.

From a letter to Carmelina
Fiera di Primiero, Italy, September 6, 1947

Mary wants us to be united on our journey! She knows that "where two or more" are united in the holy name of her Son, he is among them! (see Mt 18:20). And wherever there is Jesus, dangers flee and obstacles vanish . . . He conquers everything, because he is Love!

---

12. Historically that understanding came earlier, as can be deduced from a booklet written in the spring of 1947 by Father Leo Veuthey at the suggestion and in collaboration with Chiara, and published in the autumn of the same year, where Chiara's teaching of unity and its specific connection with Mt 18:20 is evident: see "Unità," *Messaggero di S. Antonio*, Padova, 1947.

Therefore, may today be the day of our encounter, the day of our unity.

May Mary, who takes us by the hand and unites us, fuse us more and more into one, to the point of consuming us in unity![13]

From a letter to Irene Maragliani and her friends
Fiera di Primiero, Italy, September 6, 1947

I'm convinced that she is the one who wants unity! Mary, Mother of Unity.

Our mother wants us to be saved and she wants the greatest number of souls to be saved.

She knows well Satan, his temptations, his tricks, his traps. And so she calls her children to unite and to help one another walk along the way of Love! Because where two or more unite in the name of her Son, Jesus is in their midst! (see Mt 18:20).

And wherever there is Jesus:

there is light,

love,

strength, almighty strength that will draw everyone into the Heart of God.[14]

3. A Fire That Consumes Everything

Of the letters Chiara Lubich wrote to various people between 1948-1949, those that remain are all imbued with the clear awareness that "unity is Jesus." She explicit-

---

13. Chiara Lubich, *Early Letters* (New York: New City Press, 2012), 85.
14. Ibid., 86.

ly encourages everyone to keep Jesus in their midst and emphasizes its great value. In particular, since she is in love with Jesus forsaken, she sees that the presence of the risen Christ will console Jesus, who cries out his abandonment in the men and women of our times.

Jesus among you will console Jesus who is abandoned

From a letter to Father Bonaventura da Malé, OFM Cap.
March 30, 1948

Jesus is without God. To console him, we promise to offer him always the presence of Jesus among us. "Where two or three . . . I am there."

And Jesus [in our midst] will console Jesus who cries out [in his abandonment]. My Jesus! Our Jesus![15]

From a letter to Father Valeriano Valeriani, OFM Conv., and his confreres in Assisi
Trent, Italy, April 1, 1948

Don't be afraid of anything. Be afraid only of being attached to something that is not Jesus among you. This is your Ideal and ours. Jesus among you (who also makes you present among us) is the guarantee that Jesus is within you, in the fullest unity with him! . . . Jesus crucified, who cries out, "My God, my God, why have you too forsaken me?"

It's Jesus in his greatest suffering! Infinite disunity . . . so as to give us perfect unity, which we will achieve to a certain degree here on earth and then in its fullness in heaven.

---

15. Ibid., 92-4.

Jesus, who is infinitely distressed, needs our consolation. What does Jesus need in the midst of such anguish?

What medicine can heal his pain?

God!

He is without *God*!

How do we give him God?

By being united, we will have him among us, and Jesus, who is born from our unity, will console our Crucified Love!

That is why we should increase our unity to a greater quantity of love and of souls! We want the King to grow to gigantic proportions among us! And then we'll go out seeking to recompose every disunity, especially because in every disunited soul we hear the groan, more or less loudly, of our Jesus who is crying out!

Brothers and sisters, let's love Jesus and, above all, let's be the angels of his abandonment![16]

May the whole world collapse, but may Jesus always remain among you!

From a letter to a group of men religious
April 29, 1948

Unity!

Who would dare speak of it? . . .

It is Jesus among us!

Jesus among us! To live so that we can have him always with us! To create him (understand me well) among us always, to bring him into the world that is

---

16. Ibid., 97-100.

unaware of his peace, so that we may have his light in us! His light! . . .

I'd like to talk to you about him, but I don't know how.

The heart speaks; its voice is love.

The mind contemplates, saturated with its beauty!

I would like the whole world to collapse, but that he would always remain among us, among us united in his name, because we have died to ours!

Brothers, God has given us an ideal that will be the salvation of the world! Let's remain faithful to him, whatever it may take, even if one day we were to cry out, with our souls burning with infinite pain: "My God, my God, why have you too forsaken me?"

Go ahead! Not with our own strength, meagre and weak as it is, but with the omnipotence of unity. I have seen with my own eyes that God among us accomplishes the impossible—he works miracles!

If we remain faithful to our mission ("that they may all be one") the world will see unity and with it the fullness of the kingdom of God. All will be one if we are one!

And don't be afraid to surrender everything to unity. Without loving beyond all measure, without losing our own judgment, without losing our own will and our own desires, we will never be one!

Wise is the person who dies to self so as to let God live in them! Unity is the training ground for those who fight for the real life against the false life.

Be totally united with one another. Never leave each other without having understood each other. Unity first! In everything! After everything! Discussions count for little, even the holiest of questions, if we do not give life to Jesus among us, loving one another so much that we give of ourselves totally.

I would like to tell you many things, but . . . what is the use of it? I know I am writing to my brothers in unity, and among you, everything is now like life in heaven. Each of you sees himself in the other, and rejoices!

May God bless us all and may he use us for his plan of love.[17]

Jesus throws out his net

The following letter begins with a prayer addressed to Jesus in which Chiara says: "We who have been keeping you among us for years and who have seen the miracles of your omnipotence . . ." Thus, in retrospect, Chiara recognizes the presence of Jesus in the midst of the first focolare, even before understanding explicitly Mt 18:20, which happened—as far as is documented—in September of 1947.

Here Chiara expresses her joy at the presence of Jesus in the midst of a small group of Capuchin Franciscans and hopes that he will grow and throw out his net to include many other hearts.

From a letter to Father Bonaventura da Malé, OFM Cap.
Trent, December 27, 1948

Your letter today filled me with joy.

Now, in the International College of Via Sicilia 159, there is Jesus in the midst of four hearts made into one! "Dear Jesus, Jesus of infinite love, who is

---

17. Ibid., 103-4.

among the four hearts of our brothers in Rome, receive all our joy! Seeing what you are doing, as usual we can only remain silent and adore your fathomless love! We have been living with you among us for years and have seen the miracles of your omnipotence and so we can't help but cry out to you and say, 'Grow to an infinite degree among those priestly hearts and spread the loving caress of your love in their hearts to all the souls that surround your little kingdom and gather in as many as you can.'" . . .

What a joy that Jesus—our only treasure—our only wisdom, our only joy, our only source of Life (that Life we love so much!) is among you, as he is among us! Now you don't lack anything! . . .

Your first responsibility is to ensure that all the Capuchins are one! Without excluding all the other people the Lord puts on your way.

Die, die completely in Jesus who is among you! . . .

In this way, Jesus will consume in unity, one by one, the brothers who live with you and will prepare for unity those who live far away. It's just like any object that passes close to the whirlpool in the sea or in a lake. It is irretrievably dragged into the vortex! (A whirlpool is formed when two currents come together! Isn't this also the symbol of unity?) So every soul that encounters Jesus (Jesus among us) will be irreparably lost in his love.

My wish for you is that Jesus among you will spread out his net over the whole Capuchin world and that every day there will be a miraculous catch![18]

---

18. Ibid., 134-36.

Jesus is a fire that ignites hearts

The following letter is addressed to Father Pinesi for a group of people from his parish in Pescara who are living with Jesus in their midst. The centrifugal thrust she proposes is powerful. Their goal should be to set the whole city on fire.

From a letter to Fr. Giovanni Pinesi
Rome, Italy, June 26, 1949

We received with great joy your letter with the signatures of all those living in unity. Yes, the fire is spreading on all fronts and no one can stop it. Jesus brought fire on earth, a fire that devours everything that is not God. May Jesus be in our midst and through us, bring that fire again to the world.

What a mission Jesus has given us! Just as the Father has sent him, so Jesus sends us, after having sanctified us in the truth.

The Word of Life is our hidden treasure: the one that cleanses and consumes us in one with Jesus and among us. No one will ever break that bond.

Tell the people of Pescara that we are more united to them than they can imagine. Tell them to be consumed in one, to share with one another all the treasures they possess, especially the spiritual ones, so that it will be Jesus in their midst who is made holy. Tell them to aim at the whole city, so that it will be totally conquered by Jesus who is among them if they are united.

Jesus among people works miracles. Conversions are the order of the day and more and more hearts are radically transformed. The fiery wave of charity turns everything upside down. It is the light of Jesus.

The important thing is that we remain united and that we share everything with each other as much as possible, either through our spiritual "wireless phone" as we call the communion of saints, or through all the physical means God gives us to use. May our letters spread the flame and may Jesus be glorified in the world. And if he among us is the one who glorifies himself, then the glory will indeed be great.

We conclude this chapter, which was dedicated to the discovery and practice of Jesus in the midst in the very first years of the Movement, with an excerpt from an article written by Chiara and published by Igino Giordani in the magazine Fides *in October 1948. In it, the reality of Jesus in the midst, almost unknown in the teachings and pastoral practices of the Italian Church at the time, is expressed in a very clear and solemn way, as a fundamental part of the history of the emerging Movement.*

From an article in the magazine Fides
October 1948

We understood clearly that in love we find everything, that of necessity mutual love had to be the final exhortation of Jesus to his followers and that "being consumed in one" had to be the last prayer of Jesus to his Father, as the supreme synthesis of the good news. . . .

To be consumed in one: this was the program of our life so that we could love him. But where two or more are united in his name, he is there among them. We felt his divine presence every time unity triumphed over our natural tendencies that rebelled against having to die to ourselves. We sensed the presence of his light, his love, his strength.

Jesus among us. The first small group of brothers and sisters, true disciples of his, was being formed. Jesus, the bond of unity. Jesus, king of every heart, because the life of unity presupposes the total death of our ego.

Jesus, king of that small group of souls . . .[19]

---

19. See "La Comunità Cristiana," *Fides,* October 1948: 4.

Chapter II

Jesus in the Midst Is a Person

A Real Presence, Recognizable by its Effects

It is fascinating to see how from the very beginning, Chiara described the presence of the risen Lord among those who are united in his name. He is not a concept, a doctrine, or an ideology, but rather a Person, an invisible and yet real person, who can be experienced with the senses of the soul, and who made her declare, during a meeting with young people: "If there are 700 of us here, there are not 700, but rather 701, because he is here. He is right here beside us; he understands our human condition and he loves us."

Jesus in the midst is one of the manifold ways that the risen Christ is present in his Church. He promised to be with his people "to the end of the age" (see Mt 28:20) and he is present in his ministers, in the sacraments, in his Word, in the poor, and among those who love one another, united in his name. The Fathers of the Church pointed out the truth of his presence among us, but then it was forgotten for centuries. Now the sensitivity to the presence of Christ in a united community has re-emerged. It can be found in the theological and spiritual doctrine of authentic "prophets" of our day, to the point that it can be defined as the doctrine that prepared and then characterized the Second Vatican Council.

Several years before the Council, as we have seen, the Holy Spirit led Chiara and the people who shared her spiritual adventure to live profoundly in love for one another, in accordance with the New Commandment of

Jesus. In doing so, they realized that their lives changed radically and they experienced extraordinary peace, light and <u>inner conversion</u>. These were the effects, they later understood, of the real presence of the risen Christ among them, according to the promise of Jesus: "Where two or three are gathered in my name, I am there among them" (Mt 18:20). Very soon Chiara realized that this experience was nothing other than the life of the Mystical Body put into action, an understanding which she then progressively focused on and, with the passing of time, explored more and more deeply.

1. He Is Present

"Jesus in the midst" is an expression Chiara coined to indicate a Person, and at the same time, a particular kind of presence. Jesus in the midst is the human-divine Person of the Son of God who became man, died, and rose for us. He is not only close to us, but also in us and among us when we love one another. He envelops us with his presence.

"There's a real person here!"

From a talk to a group of residents of Loppiano
Loppiano, Italy, November 27, 1975

Jesus in the midst . . . is Jesus!

It's not that here among us we have a formula or a virtue, or some goodness or kindness, or a sense of the divine. Here with us is a person! We do not see him with our own eyes, but he hears us and scrutinizes our every thought, every throb of our heart, every consent of our soul. He's here! I don't know if he is right here, or if he is over there, or there. I imagine he's within each one and envelopes us all. But he is definitely here, in person. If there are, for example, 700 of us here, there are not 700, absolutely not, but 701, because he is here.

His presence makes me tremble and almost makes me afraid to speak, because I know that he is listening to me. However, since this is also his will, I think that he is happy with what little I give him by speaking and what little you give him by listening. He lived on this earth, he knows our limitations, how small we are, how shortsighted we are. He knows us. He is not only God, which would make him unreachable, but he is also human. That's what Jesus in our midst is like.

He's worth more than any other treasure

Jesus in the midst is close to us, he knows us well and at the same time, he is God, the Son of God. The following meditation is very well known and has even been set to music and sung in various languages. In it, this precious and divine gift shines through more than any other. This is what Chiara told Bishop Montini in her meeting with him in 1953.[20]

From a meditation
1949

If we are united, Jesus is among us. And this is what is valuable. It is worth more than any other treasure

---

20. See Introduction, page 9

that our heart may possess; more than mother, father, brothers, sisters, children. It is worth more than our house, our work, or our property; more than the works of art in a great city like Rome; more than our business deals; more than nature which surrounds us with fields and flowers; more than the sea and the stars; more than our own soul.

He is the one who, inspiring his saints with his eternal truths, leaves his mark upon every age.

This too is his hour. Not so much the hour of a saint, but of him, of him among us, of him living in us as we build up—in the unity of love—his Mystical Body.

But we have to expand the presence of Christ, make him grow in other members, become like him bearers of fire. Make one of all, and in all, the One!

It is then that we live the life that he gives us, moment by moment, in charity.

The basic commandment is brotherly love. Everything is of value if it expresses sincere fraternal charity. Nothing we do is of value if there is not the feeling of love for our brothers and sisters in it. For God is a Father and in his heart he has always and only his children.[21]

The perception of the presence of Jesus in the midst, which is much more valuable than the presence of God in nature, and which Chiara had experienced through a special grace years earlier, is reflected in the following passage of her diary.

From a page of her diary
August 28, 1968

---

21. Chiara Lubich, *Essential Writings* (New York: New City Press, 2007), 102.

Yesterday, after an outing in the mountains, I came back to this little house, that Providence had given us, and I felt as if I were entering a warm little church. Whereas being up in the mountains, which we reached by cable car, and looking out at all the beauty of creation that had filled me with such joy and wonder back in 1949 and also afterwards, I realized that it didn't say anything to me anymore.

I asked myself why this was so and I think it depends on the fact that here, even though we are on vacation and resting most of the day, there is Jesus in our midst and he is the Creator of everything! Therefore, there is no comparison [between creation and the Creator]! It's obvious that this is how he wants to show himself to us now.

Those who have not yet met Christ await his presence among us

From a worldwide conference call[22]
Rocca di Papa, Italy, April 24, 1997

Yes, Jesus in our midst, the effect of unity. Not a command, or an exhortation, or a concept, or a rule, but he, he himself, a Person, who lives spiritually among those who are united in his name by love.

Today in the world in which we live, we often meet good and upright people who do not feel the need to believe in God. Some of them might even have the desire to believe, but, immersed in a world that should be Christian, and often is not, they don't find the strength

---

22. When it became possible to connect more than two telephones for a single call (the beginning of the conference calls), Chiara used to link up with as many contacts as possible among the focolare centers in the world on a regular basis.

to take the step, and so they wait, counting themselves among those who say they are searching.

Who are they waiting for?

They are waiting, perhaps unconsciously, to meet one day with Jesus. Thinking especially of these people, we see that our spirituality, and in particular the presence of Jesus, the risen Lord, in our midst is what is urgently needed and is extremely modern and timely. He in our midst is proof that he is not someone from the past, but rather is present and alive, full of light and love even today among his brothers and sisters, just as he promised when he said: "Remember, I am with you always, to the end of the age" (Mt. 28:20).

Keeping him present among us is our greatest duty. Moreover, we can fulfil this responsibility by living his commandments, which are summarized in his New Commandment, and by taking Jesus forsaken as our model of how to live it.

Meeting the living Jesus

From a page of her diary
José C. Paz, Argentina, April 19, 1998

When people encounter the Focolare Movement, they do not find a community, or a spirituality, or an organization in the Church, or a movement. They are not offered a retreat, nor a course of catechesis, nor a ritual, nor a particular atmosphere. No. Meeting the Focolare Movement is an encounter with the living Jesus! That's how we have to present our story. . .

Therefore, when a person comes into contact with the Movement, they realize that Jesus is not someone from the past, but is a reality in the present, right now.

He responds to us; he does what he promised; he is *alive*.

And the proof of this is the enthusiasm and joy that people experience and the witness he gives of himself to many.

If the Movement has been successful, and still is, with the number of its members always increasing, it is because whoever meets it, meets Jesus. And a meeting with Jesus can never be forgotten. Even if people distance themselves from him, they cannot fail to return. This is something that deeply moved us in these past few days.

2. You Can Tell His Presence by Its Effects

"To know the reality of Jesus in the midst," Chiara once said, "we have to experience it. We don't feel it with our physical senses, but rather with the senses of the soul." To explain this experience, she compares it with other spiritual phenomena, pointing out that Jesus in the midst is felt "in a higher sphere of the soul." Its effects are light, peace, joy, and strength, both for those who live it and for those who happen to encounter it. On many occasions, and in many texts, Chiara describes the effects experienced when the risen Christ is alive among those who are gathered in his name. She gives a real "phenomenology" of his presence, starting from the experience of the early years of the Movement, which was later confirmed by theologians as well as by various Fathers of the Church.

Just as we feel joy, pain, anguish and doubt, so—but in a higher part of our soul—the spiritual presence of Jesus among us gave our souls a special kind of peace that is typically his, the full joy that can only be found in him, the strength and conviction that does not come so much from our human reasoning or willpower, but from God who gives us his powerful help. . . .

His presence abundantly rewarded any sacrifice we made, justified every step we took on our journey towards him and for him, gave the right meaning to whatever happened to us and around us, comforted our pain and tempered any excessive joy.

Jesus in the midst enlightens

Jesus in the midst is light for our intelligence and for our conscience. He helps us to focus on the truths of our faith and on God's plans for individuals and for humanity. Above all, we have seen that Jesus in the midst gives us the light to understand the Scriptures and the teachings of the Church and to live them. It's "a kind of exegesis"—affirms Chiara—made by Jesus himself.

From the very beginning, it seemed to us that his presence was the reason we understood the Gospels and the Scriptures in a new way. Likewise, we feel that his presence also helped us to understand, in a deeper way than ever before, the teachings of the pope and the bishops. His presence among us also influenced our understanding of his Word. He was the one who was our master, teaching us how his words were to be understood. It was a kind of exegesis, not given by a doctor of theology, but by Christ himself.

Chiara cites Origen, a Father of the Church, to explain that this is not only an intellectual enlightenment, but one that is full of life and wisdom.

Origen says that Jesus, present among people unit-ed in his name, "is willing to enlighten the hearts of those who want to understand his teachings." He makes it clear with this statement that the enlighten-ment Jesus gives us is full of life and wisdom, influenc-ing the whole person, and not only the intellect.[23]

He is the loudspeaker of the voice of God

Jesus in the midst also enlightens our individual con-sciences so that we can understand how to act in various circumstances. Using a helpful analogy, Chiara affirms that Jesus in the midst is like a loudspeaker of God's will, of God's voice within us.

When we have no idea of what to do, to whom do we turn but to him, telling one another: "Let's put Jesus in the midst so that we can understand the will of God." He alone is the light in our lives, the solution to all our problems.

Origen already knew this because he wrote: "If we fail to resolve and explain any problem, let's approach Jesus, being in total agreement about our request, for he is present where two or three are gathered in his name and, since he is present with his power and strength, he is also willing to enlighten our hearts . . . so that with our souls we can penetrate into the heart of the issue."

From a page of her diary
New York, USA, March 31, 1964

Yesterday I was with the focolarini all day. To-day they went to work. They desire God so much and

---

23. Origen, *Comments on Matthew* XII, 15, PG 13,1131.

are so good that the supernatural union with them is tangible. In fact, at a certain moment Jesus seemed to be so present that we were deeply moved. Being with them, I understood that Jesus in the midst is like the loudspeaker of Jesus in each individual soul, that his presence magnifies his voice within us and makes us more able to perceive it, to perceive our "new self" and live it. I think this discovery is wonderful, it is new and appropriate for this city where everything has to be the biggest in the world—the widest street, the highest skyscraper, like the Empire State Building. In fact, that's where we went right afterwards, all the way up to the top of it![24]

Light for the mind also in preparing talks or texts

From a page of her diary
Loppiano, Italy, April 22, 1967

It is said that Saint Eymard used to kneel down in adoration to prepare himself before preaching. He used to say, "I make the dough and then let it bake in the Eucharistic oven."

"The Host"—someone said—"was for him a real hearth and he profited more from an hour of adoration than from a whole morning of study." Jesus in the Eucharist was his spirituality. Jesus in the midst is ours.

That is why, if we want to bear fruit when we speak, we have to prepare very well, going deep within our soul and meditating on the topic with Jesus, and in this way, develop the points of the talk.

But that's not enough. For the dough to become

---

24. Chiara Lubich, *Diary 1964/1965* (New York: New City Press, 1987), 6-7.

bread, and thus digestible for those who will listen to us, we have to bake it in the fire of Jesus in the midst.

When we share with the others in the focolare what we want to say in public, and if they listen to us giving us their full unity, Jesus in the midst corrects our talk, points out what is superfluous and can be removed, enlightens us about something to add and above all, shows us how to organize our thoughts. In this way, the talk will have a divine logic, because things said in that specific way will produce the desired effects in people, such as an inner conversion, or the confirmation of a path to follow, or an increase in love.

Thus your words will proclaim the truth and will have an impact because they will be powerful and clear.

◗ Light for the world

The previous pages have already shown how Jesus in the midst is light and fire for those who establish his presence among them by being united in his name. But he also has the same effect on anyone who encounters him present in our midst. "We soon realized that this was the real apostolate," Chiara said from very early on.[25] "It was evident that very few people could resist the impact of Jesus present in a small or large community."[26]

From "A Little Harmless Manifesto"
Trent, Italy, 1950

Christ has made us his associates in the redemption of other people, because by living in us, it is always Jesus acting in person.

---

25. "The Christian community" *Fides*, (October 1948): 4.
26. *May They All Be One* (London: New City, 1979), 75.

One by one, his words became ours. We too could say, "I am the light of the world" (Jn 8:12). In fact, from this cell of the Mystical Body that we formed, a light radiated so strongly that simple and good souls, sincerely desirous of God, like sinners humbled under the weight of their sins, recognized it as the light of Jesus. This light had such an impact on people, even those from an atheistic background, that it instantly brought about an inner conversion, in the sense that people who had been attached to a thousand things before, now felt that something else existed, something they had unconsciously yearned for, and that alone would fulfil their desires and totally satisfy them: Jesus.[27]

Jesus in the midst gives peace

The profound, supernatural peace experienced when we put into practice the command of mutual love is another sign of the presence of God, of the risen Lord among us, which we often only notice when it's missing.

From the answer to a question
from a group of seminarians
Frascati, Italy, December 29, 1975

How can we tell whether there is Jesus in the midst?

It's very simple. If Jesus is not in your midst, you feel bad. For example, three of you are working together and you try to convince yourself that there is Jesus in your midst. But you can't manage to go on, because something is not right, you feel uncomfortable. Instead, Jesus in the midst brings peace;

---

27. Chiara Lubich, *Manifesto* (London: New City, 1975), 33.

he gives you joy; you have the light. He especially brings peace, but peace is like health in our body; peace is the health of the soul. You don't feel health, you feel pain; you don't feel peace, you feel when there is no peace. So when you are in the focolare or in your nucleus, or together with someone else, or walking along the street, or at work, or in the middle of your apostolate, and you feel that there is peace, rest assured. If there is peace, there is Jesus, because he is peace. So there is no need for any particular feelings.

Jesus is a celebration

Another effect of the presence of the risen Christ is joy, supernatural joy, not the joy of this world. Sometimes it is explosive, sometimes it is interior and quiet. It is a deep joy to be shared with others.

From a worldwide conference call
Rocca di Papa, Italy, October 24, 1996

In our previous conference call, we talked about unity and said that we can live it only if we prepare to receive its grace by practicing mutual love. If we do this, unity is immediately accomplished.

This time I'd like us to look more closely at this grace, examining it a little.

What is it, who is it?

We know the answer. It is certainly not just a point of our spirituality, but rather brings among us a *person*, a person who is God himself. Unity is Jesus among us.

One of the Fathers of the Church said that unity is an "agreement" of thoughts and feelings among several people, which brings about harmony, which "unites and contains the Son of God."[28]

We can confirm that this presence is the source of profound happiness. Jesus among us is the fullness of joy, he makes of our life and of all those who live unity a continuous celebration. Why is this?

Another Father of the Church explains it when he speaks about Pentecost, after which the apostles were filled to overflowing with grace, light and joy, so much so that they seemed to be drunk. He wrote: "Although Pentecost is over, the celebration isn't over; every meeting is a celebration. Where does that come from? From the very words of Christ who said: 'Where two or three are gathered in my name, I am there among them' (Mt 18:20). Therefore," he continues, "every time Christ is present in the midst of a meeting, what greater proof do you want that it is a celebration?"[29] This is the true celebration that human hearts seek. And we are called to bring about this celebration into the midst of the world, to make the world thrill with true joy in abundance. We can do it in our small or larger communities, in our conferences, in our centers and in our little cities.

We have the duty to do it and teach others to do it, because living as "Church" means to act in such a way that Jesus and his joy are always among us. In fact, living with Jesus in the midst is not a practice that only the members of the Movement are called to do. Living with Jesus in the midst vitally inserts us into the presence of Jesus in his Church.

In fact, to explain the presence of God in the Church, the Fathers refer mainly to two passages:

---

28. Origen, *Comm. in Matth.*, XIV, 1s., PG 13.
29. John Chrysostom, *De Anima,* Sermo 5, 1, PG 54, 669.

"Where two or three are gathered in my name, I am there among them" (Mt 18:20) and "Remember, I am with you always, to the end of the age" (Mt 28:20).

May "Christopher" (bearer of Christ) be our second name during the month of November. May we be bearers of Christ in the midst of the world, not only so as to make the world smile, but also to ignite a perpetual celebration.

And to know where to start, here is a piece of advice that is the fruit of an experience I have had. Be the first to love everyone, starting right now, and teach everyone to do the same. This makes it easier for people to return our love, and it sometimes comes automatically. Thus we will have Jesus in the midst, and with him it's a celebration!

Give added joy to God

From a worldwide conference call
Mollens, Switzerland, August 26, 2004

Jesus in our midst is not something new for us. We always try to have him present in our life in common, such as in our small or large communities, and in our meetings.

We also know of his extraordinary effects, such as, for example, the recent meeting on May 8 in Stuttgart,[30] where its success was due above all to his presence. It was the same at the recent symposia we had with people of other religions, in which he spoke to the hearts of our brothers and sisters, revealing important truths to them.

---

30. A large ecumenical event of over 300 Christian movements from all

And so let's try to live with him present among us. Only in this way will what I share with you be like throwing gasoline on fire.

Yes, let's live in this way and be grateful, because Jesus in our midst will be our joy, but even more so because, through him, we can give additional joy to God in heaven. I am always impressed by the words of Theophilus, bishop of Bulgaria in 750 AD, who said: "Truly, God rejoices not in the multitude, but where two or three are gathered in his name, there is he among them."[31]

And if God rejoices—as we think—where there is unity, what greater thing can we do than to turn our lives into a series of days that add joy to the bliss that God already enjoys?

He gives us strength to face the difficulties of each day

From a commentary on the Word of Life[32]
May 2002

"Remember, I am with you always, to the end of the age" (Mt 28:20).

Jesus addresses these words to the disciples after entrusting them with the task of going into the whole world to carry his message. He was well aware that he was sending them as sheep among wolves and that they would suffer opposition and persecution.[33] That's why

---

over Europe called "Together for Europe" with the goal of reviving the Christian culture.

31. Teophilatus, *Expositio in Prophetam Oseam*, PG 126,587.

32. A monthly passage from Scripture with commentary and suggestions for how to put it into practice.

33. Mt 10:16-22.

he didn't want to leave them alone in their mission. So, just as he was leaving, he promises to stay! They will no longer see him with their eyes, they will no longer hear his voice, they will no longer be able to touch him, but he will be present among them, as before, or rather, *more* than before. If, in fact, until then his presence had been located in a specific place—in Capernaum, or on the lake, or on the mountain, or in Jerusalem—from now on, he will be with his disciples wherever they are.

Jesus had in mind also all of us who would have to live in the midst of the complex life of every day. Because he is love incarnate, he must have thought: "I want to be with them always, I want to share their concerns, I want to advise them, walk with them along the streets, enter their homes, and with my presence revive their joy." He wanted to stay with us, to make us feel his closeness, his strength and his love.

Luke's Gospel says that, after seeing him ascend to heaven, the disciples "returned to Jerusalem with great joy" (see Lk 24:52). How could that be? It was because they had experienced the truth of his words. We too will be full of joy if we truly believe in the promise of Jesus: "Remember, I am with you always, to the end of the age."

These words, the last ones Jesus addressed to his disciples, mark the end of his life on earth and at the same time the beginning of the life of the Church, in which he is present in many ways—in the Eucharist, in his Word, in his ministers (the bishops, the priests), in the poor, in the little ones, in the marginalized . . . in every neighbor.

We like to emphasize one particular presence of Jesus, the one that he himself indicated to us in the Gospel of Matthew 18:20: "Where two or three are gathered in my name, I am there among them." In this way, he can be present everywhere.

If we live what he commands, especially his New Commandment, we can also experience his presence outside the churches, among the people, wherever they live, everywhere.

What is asked of us is mutual love, which requires service, understanding and sharing in the pains, anxieties and joys of our brothers and sisters. It is the kind of love that covers over everything, forgives everything. It is the main characteristic of a Christian.

Let's live like this, so that everyone can have the opportunity of meeting him while still here on this earth.

Like the disciples at Emmaus

We find all the effects of light, joy, and strength when we look at the Gospel story of the disciples of Emmaus. During a trip to the Holy Land, in 1956, while walking along the road taken by the two disciples, Chiara thought of the similarities between the presence of Jesus in the midst and the apparition of the risen Jesus described in Luke 24:13-35.

From a talk to a group of focolarine
Grottaferrata, Italy, February 26, 1964

I cannot explain Jesus in the midst, because God cannot be explained. Over the years, I understood when he was present because I *sensed* it. I sometimes compared his presence to that of the experience of the disciples at Emmaus (see Lk 24:13-35). As you know, I went to Jerusalem to visit the Holy Land and Emmaus made a powerful impression me. It was spontaneous to compare the presence of Jesus among the two disciples and the spiritual presence . . . of Jesus among us. It is the same Jesus, even though they saw him with their own eyes and we don't see him with our own eyes, but it is the same Jesus. . . .

I remember that I was really struck by two or three things in particular, which is what led me to make the comparison between Jesus physically present with them and Jesus present in our midst. Luke says that Jesus explained the Scriptures to them. . . . And that made me recall that in the beginning of the Movement, we attributed to Jesus in our midst the fact that we understood the Gospel as we had never understood it before. Who explained it to us? Jesus in our midst! He is the one who explains the Scriptures. Then, after he broke the bread, he disappeared from them and the disciples told one another, "Weren't our hearts burning within us?" (Lk 13:32).

Now, the fire that Jesus brought on earth is not a visible fire, which might satisfy our senses. It's a spiritual fire! . . . Therefore, when people see that you are happy, that you are all very happy and that you are ready to face anything, it's because of the spiritual fire among you. It's just the opposite when a trial comes and there is no longer Jesus in the midst, and so you feel like saying: "Weren't our hearts burning within us?" Therefore, it is this burning fire in our hearts—to use human terms—that comes from the presence of Jesus in our midst, together with light, warmth, determination and strength. . . .

And then something else made an impression on me. Just as we were leaving Emmaus, the sun was setting in a golden hue and I noticed something written over the door of the house. It said: "Stay with us, Lord, because it's almost evening" (Lk 13:29). And there I re-membered that when Jesus sometimes disappears from our midst, we feel deep in our hearts just one over-whelming need: "Stay with us, Lord, because without you it is evening, and the evening is dark, it is night. Without you, our lives have no meaning, without you, we can no longer see."

He makes himself felt

From a worldwide conference call
Castel Gandolfo, Italy, December 16, 1999

In Amman[34] . . . at a certain occasion [an interreli-gious conference], I was asked how we first understood the presence of Jesus among us when we were united. In order to answer this question in total faithfulness to the Holy Spirit, I began by describing what preceded that moment in our story. I spoke about our experience of the very real possibility that we could die during a bombardment, and how we, the first focolarine, won-dered if there were something that was particularly pleasing to God so that we could live it, at least during the last few days of our lives. And so I told them about the New Commandment of Jesus, in which he asked us to love one another to the extent that he had loved us—and he laid down his life for us. In it we found the answer to our desire and immediately began to put it into practice. I told them about the pact we made, telling one another: "I am ready to die for you," "I for you," etc.

---

34. Amman, Jordan, was the site that year of the international meeting of the World Conference of Religions for Peace.

Of course, then I spent some time describing what happened after that, in the sense that we felt that our life had taken a qualitative leap, as if a net had pulled us up on high. And we experienced, for the first time, a unique peace, never experienced before (we said it then, but people still say the same now), of a light that gave meaning to everything that concerned us, of a new determination and perseverance in place of our inconsistency in putting our resolutions into practice. We were filled with a fresh, rare flooding of joy, new ardor and zeal, the fullness of life. . . .

I explained how we had wondered, in those moments, what could be the cause of all of this. And what we understood was that Jesus had made himself spiritually present among us in those moments because we were united in his name, that is, in his love. The peace, the light, the ardor, the joy, etc., were proof of it. In fact, when he is present, these are the effects. Without those effects, it is useless to delude oneself: he is not there.

Therefore, I concluded, we realized that he was present when we could *experience* him. In fact, it's not a matter of believing in him only by faith, only because he said so. No! If Jesus is among us, he makes himself felt; we can experience him.

Herein lies the beauty and the enormity of this particular presence of Jesus that we are called to live. Proof of what I am saying can also be seen when he is not present, when we don't love one another as he loved us. Then the very path we have embarked on has no meaning, the goals we have set ourselves, all that we do—our prayers, our work, our study—are all without meaning. In those moments, we walk along like people who are lame and blind, groping for something, a burden to ourselves and to others, and exposed to all kinds of temptations. There is no light, no flame, no protection, because he is not there.

You might object and say, "But we knew all this before. What's new? What do you feel that is new?" What's new is that we absolutely need to experience these effects since we are people who have taken as our "norm of norms" the presence of Jesus among us. Jesus wants—I repeat—that we be not just religious people, who believe and love him with some beautiful devotions, but people who really *know* him, who feel his presence among them. He wants us to be experts in knowing who Jesus in the midst is. And, only if we are experts in this can we be his witnesses for other people, many other people. We can truthfully tell everyone: "We have seen him with the senses of the soul; we have discovered him in the light with which he illuminates us; we have touched him in the peace that he infuses in us; we have heard his voice deep in our hearts; we have savored his unmistakable joy; we have known the heavenly fragrance of the new unwavering will he has given us." And we can assure everyone that he is happiness, the fullness of happiness.

Only those who can say these things can call themselves "a focolarino" or "a member of our Movement." We hope this is already true for many of us, since we so often hear that people notice your smiles and praise you. But we need to grow both in number and in depth. Happiness should be the heritage of as many people as possible, even of those who, at first, might seem to lack something, or even a lot, but have the most important thing—they have Jesus, Jesus in our midst.

Then, yes, our desire to make the world smile will be a success on a vast scale. What more do we want? Isn't this our religion? Jesus prayed: "May my joy be complete in them" (see Jn 17:13). He should always be among us; he should be at home with us and we with him.

This, then, is the pearl I brought back from the Middle East, a well-known pearl, but that now is even more brilliant, that is, to love one another always in such a way as to be able to testify: "I have seen him, I have heard him . . ." What a great contribution we can make to the new evangelization!

3. Among Us and in Everyone

At the end of this chapter, we consider the mystical dimension of the reality of Jesus in the midst, which reflects the mystery of the life of the Trinity. It is rooted in the doctrine of the Mystical Body of Christ, into which Christians are inserted by baptism, and by which Christ is truly present in the whole Church and in every part of it (see Rom 12:5; 1 Cor 12:12-13). This ecclesial perspective was always present for Chiara, right from the first steps in this new life (chapter 5 will deal further with this topic). Here we are including some short passages that underline the dynamic connection between the communitarian dimension of the presence of Christ among people and his presence within each individual.

Jesus in us, Jesus among us

In the following text, which describes the mystical understanding of the experience of being one soul in Christ, his soul, we come to a fuller understanding of the reality of his presence among people united in his name and also his presence within each one of them.

From her writings
August 1949

We understood that being consummated in one and basing our life's journey on *unity*, we were Jesus who journeyed. He who is Way in us became Wayfarer.

And we were no longer ourselves, but he in us: he the divine fire who consummated our two very different souls in a third soul: his own: all Fire. So we were One and Three. Jesus and Jesus in him; Jesus in me; Jesus among us. The place that received us, a ciborium with One Jesus or Three.

Jesus among us makes the beauty of each one shine out

To explain the unique quality of the new charism, Chiara drew an original comparison between her first companions gathered with Jesus among them and the friars of Saint Francis. Whereas on another occasion, she had recalled that once Saint Francis and his friars even saw Christ present among them, in this case she observes the differences between his experience and hers, without however a full assessment of the value of the Franciscan spirituality.

From her writings
Ostia, Italy, March 27, 1950

Having finished the hour of truth, we could conclude by saying: Jesus among us is: zealous like Graziella,[35] prudent like Giosi, full of light like Pasquale,

---

35. All names of the early companions of Chiara Lubich.

loving like Foco, measured like Marina, affectionate like Lia, supernatural like Antonio, simple like Marino, good-natured like Giulio, warm like Giorgio, childlike like Liliana, strong like Gisella, and so on.

Saint Francis, too, looking at his friars said: *the model friar* ought to be simple like Brother Juniper, and so on.

It can be felt that in the Franciscan Ideal there is not perfect unity. In fact, Saint Francis did not recall that the model friar is our brother Jesus.

We, the more we are consummated in one, the more we shall acquire the other's virtue (*"omnia mea tua sunt"* [all that is mine is yours]),[36] in such a way that we will be *one*, each the other, each Jesus. We will be many persons who are equal, but distinct, because the virtues in us will be clad[37] in the characteristic virtue forming our personality.

We will mirror the Trinity where the Father is distinct from the Son and the Spirit, even though within himself he contains both Son and Spirit.

The same is true of the Spirit, who contains within himself both Father and Son, and of the Son who contains within himself both Father and Holy Spirit.

The whole within each one

The reality of "the whole in each one" is described elsewhere by Chiara with the word "trinitization," referring to several souls who are "consummated in one" with Jesus in the midst and then divide to go separate ways. In this case, each carry within themselves the reality of the whole.

---

36. Jn 17:10.

37. That is, more than just clothed.

From "A Little Harmless Manifesto"
Trent, Italy, 1950

To be one for us meant to be Jesus, for all of us to be Jesus. And when we were consummated into one—and this required the perfect renunciation of our ego in every sense—and then we left one another because of having to go to work or for some other reason, we no longer brought our own spirit into the new environment (like our own way of thinking or loving or feeling, that of Graziella, or Giosi, or Livio, for example), but rather we brought the soul of Jesus, of Jesus who had been generated by our perfect fraternal communion. Each one felt they were totally Jesus.

It was as if before we had been one sacred host and then each piece carried Jesus within itself. When we came together again, the soul of each one met itself in the soul of the other and they were one.

Chapter III

The Experience of Living
With Jesus in the Midst

Jesus in the midst—as we have seen—is, first and foremost, a person, the human-divine Person of the risen Christ who, with his ascension into heaven, promised to remain with his people until the end of time. But the expression "Jesus in the midst" also means that particular manifestation of the presence of Christ linked to "two or three gathered in his name," and therefore to the mutual love that makes Christians one heart and one soul: his. This leads us to focus on the communitarian dimension of the Church, which is the Mystical Body of Christ.

How do we ensure that the presence of Christ among the members of his Body is always alive and radiant? What is the technique—so to speak—or the methodology that allows us to experience the presence of Christ among us, and to re-establish it when it fades out?

The charism of unity that characterizes the Work of Mary has proved particularly suitable for this purpose. During the first years of the Movement, Chiara and the small group around her, instructed by the Holy Spirit to put the words of the Gospel into practice, arrived at a certain practice without analyzing it too much. As the years went by, and as they experienced various problems and concrete difficulties, practical ideas developed and gradually formed a wealth of suggestions, almost a handbook for those who want to commit themselves to living with Jesus in their midst.

In numerous meetings all over the world, Chiara answered a variety of questions from people representing different vocations, social groups, and cultural backgrounds. There are audio or video recordings of all these meetings, and together with official talks, monthly conference calls, written meditations, and diaries, they form part of the legacy, or special gifts, that the members of the Work of Mary feel they first have to live, in order to then offer it to the world.

In chapter 5 of this volume, we will highlight how Chiara was always keenly aware of the continual presence of the risen Christ within his Mystical Body. However, in this chapter we would like to emphasize what she says about the special grace of his presence wherever love circulates. We would also like to present some of the advice and useful examples that Chiara gave on how to live with Jesus in the midst.

1. How to Establish
The Presence of Jesus in Our Midst

Reflecting on her experience, Chiara described some of the conditions required to fulfil this promise of Jesus: "Where two or three are gathered in my name, I am there among them" (Mt 18:20). As the theologian Yves Congar once said, this passage from Matthew represents a "covenant" relationship, a pact by which Christ is present and reveals himself in that specific way when we are united in his name. And his name, we know, is love: we have to love each other to the point of being ready to give our lives for one another. Chiara often said that Matthew 18:20 has to be understood in the light of the New Commandment:

"Love one another as I have loved you" (Jn 13:34). With these words and with the witness of his life, Jesus showed us the extent of the love required of us, which is expressed in a thousand different ways, that range from giving everything one has, to making the effort to be at one with others, to learning how to lose one's ideas out of love.

What does it mean to be united in the name of Jesus?

From a writing of 1950 used in a worldwide conference call

To be united in the name of Jesus means both to be united because of him, that is, to fulfil his commandment (which is love), and to be united in the way he wants us to be. Therefore, when we unite for a purpose that is good, even religious, but is not done in his name, he is not among us. For example: if I join a friend in the name of friendship either to do a given job or to have fun together, Jesus is not among us.

Jesus is among us when we are united in him, in his will, which means in himself, and it is his will that we love one another as he loved us.

The words of Jesus, "Where two or three are gathered in my name, I am there among them," have to be understood in the light of that other sentence of his, "Love one another as I have loved you." (Only God can understand God; and for this reason, only the Church, which has the Holy Spirit, can explain the Gospel.)

Therefore, the two of us, for example, are united in the name of Jesus if we love one another as he loved us. Now from this you will understand that we who live in the focolare do not always have Jesus among us. For this to be so, I would need to love you at all times (supposing that only the two of us are living in the focolare) as he loved us and be loved by you in the same way.

He loved us to the point of dying for us, even suffering the abandonment. Not always, and only rarely, does loving a neighbor require such sacrifice, but if the love that I give you (that expression of love) does not contain the intention of loving in this way, I do not love like him. And if you don't do the same, you don't love like him either, and so we are not united in his name and Jesus is not among us.

The conditions

In her book Jesus in the Midst, *Chiara describes the conditions required to have Jesus in the midst, confirming some passages of the Fathers of the Church, which we quote here.*

What are the conditions for having Jesus in the midst?

We know the answer. We have Jesus in our midst if we are united in his name. This means if we are united in him, in his will, in love, which is his will, in mutual love which is the supreme will of Jesus, his commandment. We have Jesus in the midst when there is unity of heart, of will and of thought, if possible in all things, but certainly in matters of faith. . . .

John Chrysostom considers that the condition for having Jesus in our midst is to love our neighbor out of love for Jesus and to love him or her as Jesus loved, and Jesus gave his life for his enemies. He takes the sentence, "Where two or three are gathered in my name, I am there among them," and asks this question. "What then? Can't we find two or three gathered in his name? Yes, but rarely. In fact, [Jesus] does not merely speak of [physical] meetings…His words have this meaning: if anyone holds me as the principal motive of their love for a neighbor, I will be with that person."[38]

We need to create the conditions

From an answer to the school for men focolarini
Grottaferrata, Italy, November 18, 1961

> *What is the condition for having Jesus in the midst? Isn't it enough to have the good will of everyone and the fact that they are in God's grace?*

No, it's not enough. Being in God's grace is not enough to have Jesus in the midst. For him to be present, it's not enough to love one another in a way that you might intend it, because love must be understood as Jesus intends it, that is, ready to give up one's life.

Now it might be that you or the others inadvertently have some small attachment to something . . . so you are not completely empty, you have not removed everything you have in your mind, your heart and your will, so that Jesus can reign among you. . . .

Jesus in the midst is a grace and this grace is Jesus who reveals himself among us. We have to create the conditions for this grace. It requires that we be completely detached from everything, love others and [love] the will of God in the present moment.

---

38. John Chrysostom, *on Matthew*, Hom. 60,3, PG 58, 587.

And what if the others don't love?

From a handwritten note in a diary
October 4, 1960

Above all else, have mutual and continuous love. Above all else. But since we can only do our part, if the other person does not respond, we still have to love above all else. We have to put into practice the motto, "Bend, but don't break."

If others don't make themselves one with us in truth, we should make ourselves one with them in love, always maintaining the bond between us. . . . The time will come—if God wants—when the bond that unites us to our neighbor will be Christ himself, Christ in our midst.

Be prepared to give up your ideas

From an answer to a group of young women in formation to become focolarine
Ala di Stura, Italy, August 12, 1963

How do you put Jesus in the midst?

To put Jesus in the midst, you need to be ready to die for everyone, "because no one has greater love than the one who gives his life for [his friends] . . ." (see Jn 15:13). And to die both physically . . . and spiritually means—and this is very important in order to have Jesus in the midst—to be ready to give up your ideas, to set aside your ideas, even your inspirations, unconditionally.

What very often stands in the way of having Jesus in the midst is our ideas, because everyone holds on to their own way of reasoning. . . .

I believe we would be sufficiently rewarded if, instead of our own petty, shortsighted, small ideas, we were to allow the spirit of Jesus, the Holy Spirit, to enter our hearts and take his place in us. Then, through us, Jesus could win back the world to God. It would be well worth the effort.

The art of putting Jesus in the midst: knowing how to lose

From a talk to the school for men and women focolarini
Loppiano, Italy, June 14, 1988

I could talk until tomorrow about how to put Jesus in the midst. . . .

I would like to touch on something that I have perhaps never shared: my experience. I am the president of the Focolare Movement—correct? And so I could sometimes, I don't know, impose my opinion and say, "No, you are not right. This is how it is . . ."

And yet my experience is that to have Jesus in the midst all the time, with serenity, with peace, and to bring ahead this Work of God, one needs to know how to lose. That is, in front of a neighbor who tells you something, even if you feel that you have a thousand objections, it is better to make yourself one with the ideas of your neighbor, if it is not a sin, because "better the less perfect in unity than the more perfect on your own."

And by the grace of God, having had some practice, I know that, even if they tell me, "This is exactly how it is," while I know very well that it's not, what difference does it make? The important thing is that there is Jesus in the midst. It doesn't matter if I know the correct version. . . .

So, knowing how to lose, knowing how to lose your idea, your position, your convictions, and make yourself one, as long as it is not a sin.

And then go ahead working for the Movement with Jesus in the midst. If that thing was true, and needs to be known, it will come out eventually. You will be able to say it at a different moment, but eventually it will come out. . . . You need to be very flexible.

. . . This doesn't mean that you become passive and you don't care about anything anymore. No, not at all. It's a passing moment that you live in that way so as not to break unity, so as not to damage unity. You do it so that everything can go ahead. We keep Jesus in our midst; he remains among us.

Ready for any contribution

To love as Jesus loved is not a matter of nice feelings, but "the constant sacrifice of our whole self to live the life of our neighbor." Among other things, living like this leads to the communion of material and spiritual goods.

How did Jesus love us? What is the measure of his love for us? Death on the cross. We too have to be ready to die for one another: "No one has greater love than this: to lay down one's life for one's friends" (Jn 15:13).

Ready, therefore, to give any gift of love, either big or small, to our neighbor, because that's what it means to give your life for someone.

Always ready to give material things . . . and so, ready to put your salary in common, as well as all the small or large possessions we have, or will have in the future. . . .

Ready to share spiritual goods, too . . . such as our own experiences, humbly offering our neighbors what seems to us to be the fruit of living our "new self" (see Rom 6:6; Eph 4:22; Col 3:9).

Spiritual openness

From a page of her diary
January 19, 1970

Another thought that keeps coming back to me in this period is the need for us to be spiritually open to one another in the focolare.

If we did nothing else every day but revive and renew, ever more deeply, this fundamental aspect of life in this work of God, we would have done enough. Truthfully!

Yes, because Jesus will then be among us and he will then enlighten us, in just a few moments, regarding the rest of the work we should do, which would have taken us hours using our own intelligence, which is so little enlightened by wisdom. Jesus is great! He pours out his providence on us in ways you would not have dreamed possible a moment before. He opens up immense opportunities for the apostolate. He teaches us how to maintain what has already been achieved and how to add luster to the works already in act. One thing is certain: he wants to work with us.

Nothing, I think, can sadden him more—if sadness could have room in his heart—than not taking him with us in an activity that directly affects him.

And perhaps nothing can cheer him up more than when we take into account his almighty contribution to the little we do.

Seeking truth together through love

Commenting on the Word of Life—"Do not let your-selves be called rabbi, because you have only one teacher and you are all students" (Mt 23:8)—Chiara reminds us that by living this sentence, we share our ideas and thus create the conditions for Jesus to be even more manifest in our midst.

November 1990

This Word of Life draws our attention to all the nuances of love that the other person expects from us: knowing how to listen patiently, offering our point of view with detachment, not behaving like teachers, but behaving like brothers and sisters who seek the truth together in love. In doing so, we will create the conditions for the true master, Jesus, to manifest himself among us always more. In fact, he said, "Where two or three are gathered in my name, I am there among them" (Mt 18:20).

2. And When He is No Longer There?

Living with Jesus in the midst is something dynamic. It requires a continuous effort. It is necessary that each person be completely and constantly "outside" of them-selves, loving God and—in God—loving others. It some-times happens that because of someone's shortcomings or an attachment to oneself, or even due to some trial that God allows, there is no longer the presence of Jesus in the midst. This may also be due to a weakening of our shared commitment. You soon realize that something's wrong. How can we remedy the situation and return to full communion with our brothers and sisters, through whom he reveals himself? Chiara, recounting her experience, and answering questions from a variety of people, explained that it is normal for these things to happen. She reminds us that we are all still "on the way" and that, while we are here on earth, we have to continually start over again.

You can't put Jesus in the midst once and for all

Just as two pieces of wood nurture a fire by being consumed, so too, if we want to live with Jesus constantly present in our midst, it is necessary to live constantly all the virtues required of us (patience, prudence, meekness, poverty, purity, etc.), so that the supernatural unity with our brothers and sisters will never weaken. It is not that we can put Jesus in our midst once and for all, because Jesus is life, he is dynamic.

When his presence begins to fade

Answer to a question from a seminarian
Frascati, Italy, December 29, 1975

Jesus assured us that he would be present among those who are united in his name and we have understood the fundamental importance of his presence in the Christian community as a result of love fully circulating among us. But what can you do when this is not the case and everything seems to crumble?

This is the experience everyone has when we begin to live our evangelical spirituality. After the first period characterized by special graces from God, we no longer feel a great enthusiasm in loving God with our whole heart, soul and strength and in loving our neighbor. We are no longer ready to give our lives for each other as we were before. We could say that we have given a lot, but not everything. And so unity among us starts to fade.

In moments like this, we cannot be at peace, because we cannot live without Jesus; our Christian community has no meaning if Jesus is not among us. We have to be like a person who is drowning. They grab hold of anything they can find to save themselves. We have to use any means suggested by the Gospel in order to recompose unity.

If the lack of unity was caused by the behavior of someone else, then we have to double our love towards that person, without making them feel that we are pressuring them to change, but rather helping them, in all the thousands of ways love suggests to us, to start loving again. If, instead, it was our fault, we have to immediately get up on our feet again, renew our choice of God, and start again to love the others. We have to admit our failure and put things right. We have to tell one another that we don't want to live even one moment without Jesus in our midst.

Eternally starting again

From a handwritten note in her diary
October 10, 1965

"As I have loved you." This is the pact we focolarini made when we entered the focolare. If we had always implemented it, even 50% of the time, how many more fruits would have been produced by the Movement, and perhaps some vocations would have been saved!

Who among us really died for their brother or sister? And if we had to endure something, how many times did we have a long face? What a stumbling block for the presence of Jesus in the midst, what an inconsistency! But you can always start again (as long as you are alive!). We have to start again always. It is in this eternal "starting again" that will ensure that the Movement will continue to develop, and will avoid those inevitable declines (as some say), which however cannot happen if Jesus is among us, because he is life.

3. The Radical Choice That Love Requires

From what has been said so far, we understand that the love needed to maintain the life of Jesus in our midst is not just any kind of love, but is radical, rooted in God. This can be accomplished by living two points of the spirituality: "making ourselves one" with our neighbor and, in order to be able to do this, the personal love for Jesus forsaken. The first, "making ourselves one," requires, on the one hand, being empty of ourselves in order to welcome the other person, which is a necessary condition for a profound communion, and on the other hand, requires "entering" into our neighbor in order to take upon ourselves their burdens, joys, and sorrows. To do so requires, Chiara says, the death of oneself, the crucifixion of one's ego. The second point to live, "Jesus forsaken," refers to the cry of Jesus on the cross: "My God, my God, why have you forsaken me?" (see Mt 27:46; Mk 15:34). We need to embrace him, who was abandoned and then rose, in every situation in which we suffer or are at the end of our strength. In this way, we will not be turned inwards on ourselves, but rather projected outwards in love, as has been amply illustrated in a previous book in this series.[39] To make ourselves one and to love Jesus forsaken are, therefore, two key factors for establishing and keeping Jesus in our midst in all our various forms of community life and in lighting up new cells of his presence everywhere throughout the world.

To enter into our neighbor's life

*From an answer to the community
of the Movement in Rome*
Marino, Italy, April 9, 2000

> *Chiara, the unity of which you speak has its roots in God and in the Trinity from which it derives. It can inspire our daily life, and our concrete daily activities. Can you tell us more about this?*

We certainly should live according to the model of the most holy Trinity. When is it possible to live like this? When Jesus is among us.

And how can we have Jesus among us? How can we be certain that he is in our midst? We have to love one another as he loved us. . . . How did he love us? He loved us to the point of dying for us. So we need to understand what it means to die. I have to love you, being ready to die for you, but not only with an intention to do it if I had to, thinking, "If I were asked, I would give up my life." No, you really have to die now. So for me to really love you means that I do not exist, that I

---

39. Hubertus Blaumeiser, ed., *Jesus Forsaken* (New York: New City Press, 2016).

am nothing, that I try to enter into your life. I have to try to understand you, to understand your joys, your sufferings, your problems, to take in everything about you. And you have to do the same with me.

I *am* love only by being nothing, like Jesus forsaken, only if I die to myself, only if I am truly nothing. But if I am love, I am Jesus. Therefore, in order to have Jesus in our midst, it is necessary that, first, we have Jesus within us. We have to *be* Jesus first, we have to be dead to ourselves first, and then mutual love is triggered, and when mutual love is triggered, Jesus is in our midst.

But you might say, "What difference is there between Jesus before and Jesus afterwards, when he is in our midst, and therefore also in each one of us?" He's more fully present when he is among us. You'll ask me, "But can Jesus be more or less full?" Of course he can! Jesus in the heart of Saint Therese of the Child Jesus is certainly a much fuller presence than in any of our hearts. Therefore, we have to love each other in this way, always ready to die, to "be" Jesus first, and be Jesus also afterwards when he is in our midst. And we realize when he is (among us) because we experience peace, tranquility, serenity, ardor, and the desire to do things. This is the dynamism of the Christian life. It's life according to the model of the Trinity.

Full amnesty

From a worldwide conference call
Rocca di Papa, Italy, October 15, 1981

What I would like to stress today for all of you is *unity*. Unity has to triumph: unity with God, unity among all men and women on earth. And what is the way to do this? We have to love everyone with the merciful love that was characteristic of our life in the early days of the Movement. In fact, we decided that when we woke up every morning, and throughout the day, we would see all the neighbors we met—in our families, at school, at work, everywhere—as new, totally new. We saw them like that, not remembering anything about their faults or failures, but rather covering over everything with love. To love just as the Word of Life this month suggests to us, "Forgive seventy times seven" (see Mt 18:22). To approach everyone with complete amnesty in our hearts, forgiving everyone and everything.

And then, to make ourselves one with them in everything but sin, in everything except evil. Why is that? Because we want to obtain that wonderful result to which the apostle Paul aspired. He said that he made himself all things to all people "so as to gain the greatest number for Christ" (see 1 Cor 9:19). So, if we make ourselves one with others, helped by this effort to forgive everything, we can pass on our Ideal to them. And, once this is achieved, we can establish the presence of Jesus in the midst with them, Jesus, the risen Lord, Jesus, who promised to be always with us in his Church, and who in some way allows himself to be seen and heard when he is in our midst.

This has to be our main task: to live in such a way that Jesus lives among us, he who is the conqueror of the world. If we are one, in fact, many will be one and the world will one day see unity. And so, let's establish cells of unity everywhere: in our own families, in our apartment building, with those with whom we work, study or play, with everyone, as much as possible, to light these fires everywhere. We have to concentrate all our efforts on this, because to love in this way, and reach the point of having this result, requires sacrifice, self-denial, renunciation, losing and bombarding our own will in order to do the will of our neighbor.

The new direction we need to give our Movement in the world is precisely this: to light up fires, to make sure that Jesus in the midst is alive everywhere.

Jesus in the midst is a fruit of the love for Jesus forsaken

From a reply to the residents of Loppiano
Loppiano, Italy, November 27, 1975

> *What is the relationship between Jesus in the midst and Jesus forsaken?*

The relationship between Jesus in the midst—we hope he is present here now—and Jesus forsaken is the relationship between the means and the end, that is, Jesus forsaken is the necessary means to reach Jesus in the midst. Just as Jesus redeemed humanity through his abandonment, in the sense that he united all of us, his children, with the Father, and was the means by which he brought about unity, so Jesus forsaken, loved by us, brings about Jesus in the midst, gives birth to him, makes him live among us.

In particular moments of suffering

In the following telephone message, Chiara explains that whereas the love required to live with Jesus in the midst is generally "an easy yoke and a light burden" (see Mt 11: 30), there can be some exceptions.

From a worldwide conference call
Rocca di Papa, Italy, April 24, 1997

There can be moments, however, when it is difficult to call the yoke of the Lord light and easy. At times, for example, health issues keep us from being "up" and can even affect our souls, making us close in on ourselves and feel almost incapable of relating to others.

Or at times you are obliged to keep certain secrets that actually weigh you down. It would be a relief to communicate them, but you cannot. They may concern ourselves—like trials of our souls—or others, like sad or delicate facts that have been confided to us in secret.

Or there might be moments when we are overwhelmed by temptations that can only be told to a priest. Or we might experience the sudden death of someone dear to us, or a terrible accident that leaves us in anguish, and we think that others cannot possibly understand our feelings.

Or we might learn that we have a serious illness, which could be fatal . . .

Or . . . or . . .

These are all painful circumstances that God allows so that he can work on us, using the instrument that can't be ignored, and that Jesus himself experienced: the cross.

How should we act in these situations?

We can try to rejoice, at least with our will, so as to be a little bit like Jesus. Although he felt abandoned, he cast every anxiety into the heart of the Father (see 1 Pt 5:7).

We need to continually offer everything, helped by the grace of the moment, which will not fail us, until the time comes when God gives peace back to our tormented soul.

But keep in mind that we always have to continue loving others—of course, as much as is possible for us in those situations—and confide in them, at least in a general way. Tell them, for example, "I'm going through a trial . . ." Say it out of love, so that the communion among you remains alive and doesn't diminish. Besides, this kind of communication is always the best tonic for us in every situation. Thus, Jesus among us—if we do not stop "generating" him, as Paul VI said[40]—will lift us up even in those difficult moments and he will show us, always and everywhere, that his yoke is easy and his burden light.

How to resist the enticements of the world

From an answer to a volunteer[41] *in Loppiano*
Loppiano, Italy, May 12, 1987

> *We would like to be more radical in our choice of God and implement a communion of goods that is more in keeping with our vocation. We are immersed in the world, living in many different social contexts. How can we find the balance between being prudent when necessary and yet trusting in providence?*

We need to walk on two legs. The two legs are Jesus within us, the risen Lord—who shines out when we

---

40. To the Parish of Saint Mary the Comforter, Casal Bertone (Rome), 8 March 1964, in *Insegnamenti di Paolo VI*, Poliglotta Vaticana, II, 1964: 1073.

41. The Volunteers of God are lay people committed to the aims of the Focolare Movement and to bringing God back into the heart of society. They meet in a nucleus, which should be a "temporary focolare."

embrace Jesus forsaken—and Jesus among us. We cannot walk with only one leg. . . . You might wonder why it is so necessary to put Jesus in our midst. It's because we *are* immersed in the world and the world belongs to the devil, who is the prince of this world. Besides this, the world itself is full of allurements, materialistic values and secularism.

You *can* manage to go ahead on your own—it is possible, but at a certain moment, you will collapse. Why is that? Because everything around you is much more powerful. You have to reinforce yourself, and as we know, two friends together, two people who are united with one another are like a fortified tower (Prv 18:19). You have to be as strong as that.

That's why Mary invented this spirituality and the Holy Spirit gave it to us. It's a way of life in which it's necessary to live with the risen Lord within us and also among us. We need to have both of them; we cannot go ahead without them. Sooner or later, we will surrender to a merely human, if not evil, way of life. We will give in to human reasoning, to a human way of thinking. . . . So we need to journey with Jesus in the midst. . . .

These two elements—the risen Jesus within us and the risen Jesus among us—are essential for us. They are necessary for our sanctification. We cannot become holy by ourselves. We have to become holy together. Ours is a collective way to holiness. The presence of Jesus in the midst is essential, because—I repeat—by ourselves we cannot do it. We've had 40 years of experience now and we have seen that we really can't go ahead on our own.

We also need to have Jesus in the midst in order to build up the Movement, to work for the Movement. Otherwise who knows what might come out, who knows what kind of spirituality would develop, who knows what strange inspirations would emerge! While with Jesus in the midst, you can validate everything and confirm that it is authentic.

4. To Keep the Presence of the Risen Lord Among Us

In addition to the effort to make ourselves one with our neighbors and to love Jesus crucified and forsaken, Chiara points out various ways of keeping Jesus in the midst in everyday life, when the "dust" of familiarity clouds the relationships among us, or when we get to know too well the limitations and habits of those close to us, and this too becomes an obstacle to unity. Instead it is necessary to see each other new every day. This can be facilitated by using the "pact of mercy," that is, seeing others as if we were meeting them for the very first time, maintaining a "supernatural" gaze, seeing Jesus in others. It will also be useful to remind one another of our commitment to live mutual love, saying, for example: "Let's keep Jesus in our midst." Finally, each one should remember not to "lean" on Jesus in the midst, depending on the others and just enjoying the unity, but rather giving their own personal contribution of love.

When the "dust" of familiarity interferes with our unity

Fraternal communion, however, does not mean being in a perpetual state of bliss. It is a continual conquest, with the result that we not only maintain the communion among us, but also spread it to many other people, because the communion we are speaking about is love, it is charity, and charity is diffusive by its very nature.

How many times, among people who have decided to go to God together, unity weakens, the "dust" of familiarity accumulates between one soul and the other. The enchantment fades, because the light, which had been shining among them, slowly starts to dim! This "dust" is caused by a certain attitude or an attachment of the heart to oneself or to other people, or loving oneself for oneself and not for God, or loving one's neighbors for themselves and not for God. At other times, it is because one withdraws from others instead of being directed towards them, and focuses on self, on one's own will, and not on God, on their neighbor for God, and on God's will.

Or very often it occurs because of an inaccurate judgment of someone we live with. We had said that we wanted to see only Jesus in our neighbor, deal only with Jesus in our neighbor, love Jesus in our neighbor, but now we notice that our neighbor has this or that defect, this or that imperfection. Our sight is clouded; our soul is no longer full of light. As a result, we cause a breakdown of unity, which is our fault.

Maybe it's true that our neighbor, like all of us, did something wrong. But how does God see them now? What is the truth about them, what is the real state of their soul? If that person has been reconciled with God, then God no longer remembers anything; he erased everything with his blood. So why should we remember their wrongdoing? . . .

Charity is maintained with truth and truth is pure mercy, with which we must be clothed from head to toe in order to call ourselves Christians.[42]

Making it easy for Jesus to live among us

From a worldwide conference call
Rocca di Papa, Italy, June 3, 1982

If we knew that a special guest had decided to come and live in our house for a while, we would certainly be careful that they find the door open. We would prepare everything well and arrange everything in the best way for them.

Now we know that Jesus himself is with us every day until the end of the world. And so, what should we do about it? I think the first thing would be to identify where he might be. We know that he is present here on earth in the Eucharist, in the poor, in those who act and speak in his name, in his Word, in each one of us through grace. . . .

But this year we understood that he wants the members of our Movement to discover him in one place in particular: in their midst. That's what he wants; this is his desire. In fact, we could say that one of his goals in bringing about the Movement was to be able to establish his presence everywhere, also outside of the churches, among the people, in the places where they live, wherever they are.

So let's make room for him among us, especially among the people entrusted to us, in what we call our

---

42. Chiara Lubich, *Meditations* (London: New City, 2005), 102-4.

"grape bunch."[43] From there, he can radiate love and light to many other people in the world. We need to renew our commitment to serve others and to make ourselves one with each other, and in this way, we will make it easy for him to live among us, we will make it possible.

May he always reign among us. May he remain with us, and if so, we can be with him, at least for this next two weeks. We couldn't wish for a better friend for our journey. And we certainly cannot measure the effects of this divine company.

Therefore, a useful motto for the next few weeks is: "Make it easy for Jesus to live among us."

Tell each other, "Let's keep Jesus in our midst"

From an answer to young people in formation to become focolarini
Rocca di Papa, Italy, June 27, 1990

> *Some time ago, speaking to the men religious, you said that Jesus in the midst is not a democracy. Could you expand on this so that we can always keep Jesus in the midst in the focolare?*

Democracy means that the majority rules. It is the majority that counts; the person who gets even just fifty-one votes (out of a hundred) wins. But, in our case, the majority doesn't rule. In our case, it is Jesus in our midst who is important, that is, the unity among us all, the consensus of everyone. However, since the Church,

---

43. Members of the Movement share the spirituality with small groups of people, who are in close contact with one another, like bunches of grapes on a vine.

of course, foresees that sometimes there might be some difficulties, as for example, a dispute during the General Assembly, it states that "at least two-thirds have to agree." And we put it [in the Statutes], because two-thirds is a good amount; it is more than the majority. But this rule applies when there are some people living their "old" self (see Eph 4:22-24). Instead, the ideal for us is always unanimity.

You have to do all that is necessary to keep Jesus in the midst always. You need to declare it, saying it aloud, whereas sometimes we are embarrassed about saying it to another person, actually telling them: "Let's keep Jesus in our midst." [But even if] you don't think it's the right time to mention it . . . do it just the same. Declare it to one another, because if he is not there, nothing has value, everything is empty. . . .

Just this morning I was studying our Statutes and I thought: "What guarantees that things will go on even when I am no longer here?" The answer is obvious: it will be Jesus in the midst. That's how it has always been.

A useful technique

From an answer to young people in formation
to become focolarini
Rocca di Papa, Italy, December 30, 1975

> *Sometimes it's difficult to be truly united in the name of Jesus. Can we use Christian violence to ensure his presence among us?*

I'd say it's a good idea to use violence against ourselves, against our own ego, also in order to establish the conditions that will allow us to merit the presence of Jesus in our midst. This is the only kind of violence we should use—against ourselves. In the early days of our experience, my companions and I used techniques that might still be useful today. For example, we made a kind of pact, promising to see one another new every day, as if we were meeting for the very first time, without remembering the faults of the previous day. We called it the "pact of mercy."

And in the evening, before going to bed, we buried all the impressions we had of the others' shortcomings or any judgments about what we had noticed in the people with whom we lived. We would wake up the next morning and see everyone as new, as if they had never had any flaws. That was a form of violence, wasn't it? Because it was like killing the idea we had in our heads of the others, so as to help us see only Jesus in each person.

Not mere friendship

*From an answer at a conference of people
who work in parishes*
Castelgandolfo, Italy, March 4, 1989

> *How can we maintain a deep spiritual relationship with each other when we are so used to being together that we run the risk that the relationship among us is merely a nice friendship?*

This is one of the defects that can happen. . . . And so, the love that had been based on a divine motive disappears, and our relationship becomes merely human, it becomes just friendship. . . .

You have to do something about that, of course. And you need to make up for it by bringing God into all your relationships. . . . You have to see Jesus (in others) and maintain the relationship between you and Jesus in the others. You know that at the end of your life, the Lord will tell you: "I was hungry, I was thirsty, I needed advice, I needed comfort, I needed to be cheered up, and you did it to me" (see Mt 25:35). He'll say this because we did those things to another person.

A relationship just as friends is absolutely not enough for us. There's no doubt about it. It's obligatory that we always strive for a supernatural relationship. We absolutely have to see Jesus in the other person. . . . In this way, when two of us love one another in God, we establish Jesus in our midst . . .

And just think that we cannot lean even on Jesus in the midst. To have Jesus in the midst is wonderful! We feel so much joy, peace, ardor, trust, but we cannot lean on him. We always have to be aware of who is with us and be attentive to him. We shouldn't become people who exploit Jesus in the midst. In fact, in our Movement, we consecrate ourselves to Jesus forsaken, not to Jesus in the midst, and therefore to any kind of suffering, to people far from God, to people in crisis, to people in need.

Therefore, we go to our meetings, where there is Jesus in the midst, in order to be renewed, but then we always go out to face the difficulties of the world, because that's where Jesus forsaken is waiting for us.

Be fully charged

*From an answer to the men and women focolarini
of Loppiano*
Loppiano, Italy, May 16, 1987

> *What would you suggest to us so that we can have
> the greatest possible presence of Jesus among us at all
> times?*

You need to go to your focolare already "charged"
with love, not with the desire of being filled by Jesus
in the midst. In order to arrive "fully charged" in the
focolare and thus able to give your contribution (because Jesus is not in the midst if your contribution is
missing), you have to love your neighbors all day long.

I have noticed that, if I see Jesus in everyone I meet
during the day while doing the will of God, then as
soon as I see Gis or Oreste or Chiaretto, it's always a
celebration for us. This means that we immediately
establish Jesus in our midst. But we have to arrive in
focolare already being Jesus, so that he can be fully in
our midst.

Having the risen Lord already within us

From an answer to a group of volunteers
Castel Gandolfo, Italy, January 27, 1987

> *In the life of unity in the nuclei, we are aware of our
> limitations. Sometimes, even for those of us who are
> very generous and always give of themselves, it is diffi-
> cult to understand the requirements of the life of unity.
> What do you suggest so that there is always this living
> flame among us, which we can then show to the world?*

This is a very important point, because, even if there are generous people, but who do not give the right importance to unity, it is a problem. To tell you the truth, sometimes I am a bit worried about some of the nuclei. I know that they are temporary focolares, not permanent focolares, and so I am concerned about whether they have enough time to establish the presence of Jesus in the midst.

Therefore, my advice is this: go to the nucleus with the risen Lord already within you, ready to help the others, so that you can have Jesus in the midst. However, even when you are perhaps going through a trial—and who knows what kind of trials the Lord might send you—and you go to the meeting to ask for help, that's okay. Even if the whole nucleus meeting consists in re-establishing the presence of Jesus in the midst, for me that is enough. It's enough, because later, you can make a phone call to arrange all the practical details. It can all be done quickly with just a simple phone call. The important thing is to put Jesus in the midst—this is the basis of everything. In our Movement, without him, we have nothing.

Launch into loving

In the following answer, Chiara gives practical advice on how Jesus in our midst during a meeting with our brothers and sisters can remain alive in us and illuminate our lives when we go our separate ways.

Answer to a volunteer at a conference of members of the Movement in northern Italy
Rimini, Italy, September 23, 1997

Can you give us advice so that the unity established in the nucleus meeting can remain alive in us and be a light for us, especially when we risk falling back into an individualistic way of life?

In this case, you need experience, you need to practice, you really have to be determined, because in the nucleus you are helped by the others and with them we can have Jesus in the midst. Instead, when you leave the meeting, you are alone. What should you do?

There is a motto that we tell everyone all over the world: "You, Lord, are my only good" (see Ps 16:2). When we feel that the atmosphere of unity is diminishing, that the light is growing dim, we go deep into our hearts and tell Jesus . . . "This is you, Lord. I offer you this suffering." . . . And then launch into loving and the light returns.

What is this light? It's the risen Lord who shines out once more in us, and he is the one who leads us to love everyone, because his new law is within us, the law of love. Therefore, we will love not only the volunteers of our nucleus, but also our son, our friends, those who work with us—we will love everyone. Some people will respond to our love and express the desire to love in the same way, and so we can introduce them to this new way of life and put Jesus in the midst with them, too.

Therefore, in the future, you will have unity in the nucleus, but also outside in the world, perhaps with a child who understands our Ideal and wants to be united with you in the name of Jesus.

5. The Dynamics of Living with Jesus among Us

In the preceding texts there seems to be a paradox: we have to be Christ in order to love our neighbor with his love and thus establish the presence of Jesus among us, but we are not perfectly Christ until he is in our midst. It is "a before that is also an after," Chiara affirms, "a mystery that is very easy to live but cannot be grasped with human reasoning." By analogy, the mystery of the holy Trinity might enlighten us on how there can be two co-essential dimensions: each person is Christ, due to baptism which inserts them into the Church, and is Christ to the full when they are "one" as part of the Mystical Body.

The ascetical and mystical aspects of a collective life

From an answer to the members of the Movement from Poland, Lithuania, and Russia
March 5, 2000

> *Can you give us the key that will enable us to live unity as it is in the Trinity? What are the ascetical and mystical aspects of this life in communion with others?*

It is not enough to be united just in any way to have Jesus in our midst. For example, two missionaries might tell one another: "Let's both go to Angola." Perhaps they help each other to get ready. For example, one of them brings certain things that will be useful and the other gets other things, and then they leave. Just doing these things together does not mean that they have Jesus in the midst.

To have Jesus in the midst one has to live according to the life of the most holy Trinity. How does one do that? I'll tell you something very beautiful. Look at the life of the Trinity. The Father generates the Son; the Son loves the Father in return; the Holy Spirit proceeds as the third Person. The Holy Spirit is third. However, if we think of God from all eternity, the Holy Spirit has always been there; one cannot think of an isolated Father, an isolated Son. The Holy Spirit has always been there. One could say in human words that the Holy Spirit was there before and comes after, as the third Person.

To live well with Jesus in the midst it's necessary that first Jesus be present in us, before establishing unity, and also afterwards, with the difference that before he is a Jesus of a certain fullness, and afterwards he is fully Jesus, the Jesus of the Mystical Body, when all its members are united. So, how do you live Jesus first? By being Jesus. You have to be Jesus. This is the ascetical aspect because our effort is required, that is, we have to *be* love, and this means losing everything of ourselves for others, living the other person, loving them by not existing for ourselves, because only if we "are not," we "are" Jesus. . . . This is the ascetical aspect. What does this mean? It means that it requires our effort.

Then you love and are loved in return. What happens then? We discover the same things that happened during the early days. We start to feel happy, we have the light, everything has meaning, we sense a new determination, we feel that Jesus is in our midst. It's something you sense, just as you also realize when Jesus is not in our midst, which is terrible. When there is Jesus in the midst, you experience peace; you feel it. Why is this? What happened? It's because in loving one another, we receive the grace of unity, which Jesus asked of his Father: "Father, may they all be one" (Jn 17:21). In fact, Jesus never asked us for unity. He commanded us to love, yes, but not to create unity. He asked the Father for unity. Unity is a grace that has to come from God, and when it comes down, we have Jesus in the midst. This is the mystical aspect—mystical means an action of God, means experiencing God. And for us, in this century, it is very important to experience, to feel if it is there or if it is not. This is very important.

Karl Rahner, the well-known German theologian, stated, I believe, that in this third millennium Christians need to be mystics or else they will not be Christians. Why, I wonder, would Rahner say that? And I explained it to myself by thinking that there is so much materialism in the world, and people only value and accept what they can see and touch. Therefore, the Lord sent on earth a spirituality in which even what is divine can in some way be touched. . . . If there is Jesus in the midst, one feels it, one touches it with the senses of the soul.

Therefore, we have to be Jesus first, just as the Holy Spirit was always within the Trinity, and also afterwards, as the fruit of our mutual love. This is the mystical aspect, our mystical life. And so, in our spirituality, even from a very young age, we already live both the ascetical and mystical aspects. . . . This is the great originality of our life. This is our mysticism, our asceticism, not that of the individual spiritualities. Ours is a collective way.

Being totally active and totally passive

In the following passage, taken from Chiara's mystical writings, what emerges is the dynamic of being together with others to form one single Jesus, by living with Jesus in the midst. And at the same time, each one is distinctly another Christ. The text then presents another apparent paradox: to live with Jesus in the midst everyone has to be totally active (by loving) and totally passive (because his presence is a gift). It is the unity of opposites which is God.

From her writings
Most likely in 1950

When we are united and he is there, then we are no longer two but *one*. In fact, what I say is not said by me, but it is I, Jesus, and you in me who say it. And when you speak it is not you, but you, Jesus, and I in you. We are a single Jesus and also distinct: I (with you in me and Jesus), you (with me in you and Jesus), Jesus among us in whom I and you are. . .

The new thing in this light (which is a newness of practice) is that not only should we not be, we cannot be parasites of Jesus among us and beautify ourselves with him, passively awaiting his light. In fact, he is not among us if we are not him. We must therefore put all we do into being him, but wait passively for him to be among us in order to be him.

From this we see the splendid simplicity of our Ideal that is, however, also divine and mysterious.

To live Christianity means all of us being active and all of us being passive: the unity of opposites: *God*.

Chapter IV

Jesus in the Midst
and the Work of Mary

Giving Jesus to the World

Jesus in the midst can be lived by everyone, and the charism of unity, which is inherently bound to it, is a gift to the whole Church and, consequently, to all of humanity. However, it is also true that to activate and spread this gift, God used the same method he has always used throughout the centuries to bestow on humanity a particular charism. He chose one particular part of his people, a small community that then formed a specific work within the Church. This work, whose founder is Chiara Lubich, is the Focolare Movement, also known as the Work of Mary, which is the official name given to it when it was approved by the Catholic Church in 1962. It is a name that indicates a goal to achieve, which is to give, like Mary, Jesus to the world.

Chiara always said that the true founder of this Work is not a human person, but rather Jesus in the midst of its members. He is the one who sustained and guided it to open new and unexpected pathways. He was the author of the Statutes that govern it, and he will be the one who will guarantee that everything goes ahead in the future, according to God's plans, even now that Chiara is no longer physically present.

Jesus in the midst constitutes the life of the small communities, called "focolares," and also of every gathering, both large and small, of members of the Movement. As reported on the first page of its Statutes, Jesus in the midst is the "norm of norms" to be put before any other idea or activity.

The novelty of this approach is that one does not go to God alone, but together with others. Indeed, those who live this spirituality seek God not solely in their own hearts, but, in particular, in the relationship with their brothers and sisters. The "interior castle" discovered and illustrated by Saint Teresa of Avila has a "natural" correspondent in the "exterior castle," built by the presence of Jesus in the midst.

1. Jesus in the Midst:
The Vocation of the Work of Mary

The first focolare was simply called "la casetta" (the little house). It was an apartment, located in Piazza Cappuccini in Trent, and had been offered to Chiara and some of her first companions because of the lack of housing during the war. Nothing written has survived from that time to record the life with Jesus in the midst in that first focolare, but there are some observations made by Igino Giordani, who met Chiara on September 17, 1948. He wrote that the life with Jesus in the midst was already shared by all those who lived the spirit of the focolare. He wrote: "It was their norm, and it still remains the norm, not only of its community life, but also of every meeting promoted by the focolare. When two focolarine, or two people who live its spirit, are together, the first thing they do is to put Jesus in the midst. They are united in him so that in whatever they say, or plan or decide, it is Jesus who speaks, and Jesus who decides. They conform their life to the Gospel." This distinctive element continues to characterize the Movement in every area and every aspect. It is a commitment that needs to be renewed continuously, because otherwise nothing has meaning.

The premise to every other rule

The premise to the General Statutes of the Work of Mary given below expresses the fundamental role of the presence of Jesus in the midst for the whole Work of Mary. It repeats a page already present in the first and provisional General Statutes, which were approved by the Catholic Church in 1962.

From the General Statutes of the Work of Mary
June 29, 1990

> Mutual and constant love,
> which makes unity possible
> and brings the presence
> of Jesus among all,
> is, for those who are part of the Work of Mary,
> the basis of their life
> under every aspect:
> it is the norm of norms,
> the premise to every other rule.

You cannot be without his presence

From a worldwide conference call
Castel Gandolfo, Italy, April 29, 1999

For more than fifty years I have been telling you, and myself, that the "norm of norms," and therefore, even the basis of our prayer life, is unity. And yet, we always need to renew this obligation, we always have to start over again. . . .

Dear friends, let's make every effort never to forget this, or better, never to forget Jesus, who has to come before all else. Jesus in the midst is the new and unique gift we are called to offer the world.

What a great honor it is to be able to live this vocation! What immense joy it gives us!

Ours is the Work of *Mary*; it is Mary's in the sense that it is hers. But, if this Work is hers, then so are *we*, each one of us, individually. We belong to her. In fact, we each have to be another little Mary. And this is precisely the role of our spirituality. It makes it possible for us to relive her in some way, here on earth, by imitating her.

As we know, Mary is a person who is highly privileged. She was immaculate from her conception; she has been assumed into heaven; she is the queen of the universe. But more than anything else her greatness lies in her divine motherhood. She can say "my son" to the Incarnate Word in her womb, just as the heavenly Father says it to the Word in the bosom of the Trinity. It is a prerogative of hers that will never be understood enough.

Yet it is precisely in her motherhood that we can, in our own way, imitate her, by living in such a way that Jesus is always "generated" among us by our mutual love. And to imitate Mary in her divine motherhood is certainly more possible for those who follow a communitarian spirituality, like ours.

Therefore, let's always focus our attention on being a living expression of our characteristic vocation. People might ask us: "Who are the focolarini?" or "Who are the members of the Focolare Movement?" If so, we can answer: "They are people who always offer Jesus to the world in a very real way, so that, as in the past, he can continue to enlighten, instruct and guide the world along the right paths. He brings to life and increases a people that belongs only to him and will direct humanity towards accomplishing universal brotherhood."

We who belong to the Focolare Movement cannot live without him being present among us. Our life would have no meaning. We would be betraying God's call.

What is our path?

From a talk with a group of young people interested in becoming focolarini
June 1, 1958

When Jesus first chose each of us and when we responded to him by choosing God, he could have used us to bring about any number of good things. For example, he could have formed us as people who spread Eucharistic devotion all over the world, people who spread everywhere the importance of adoring God. God is here on earth, and so why aren't all of us adoring Jesus in the Eucharist for hours and hours, even all night long? It's because this isn't what Jesus wanted from us.

Or he could have asked us to become Bible scholars, people who study the Scriptures, but he didn't. He could have asked us to look inwards, into the "interior castle" of our soul, and become contemplatives, but that's not what Jesus wanted either.

He could have launched us into the world to spread the practice of the fourteen works of mercy, like feeding the hungry, giving water to those who need it, and many other things that the works of mercy teach us to do. But Jesus didn't want even this from us.

When he taught us to take God as the Ideal of our lives, he made us understand: "If you want to find him, you will find him in your midst. Love one another and, by loving one another, I will be in your midst, because where two or three are gathered in my name, I am there among them."

Therefore, where do we have to find God? Which aspect of divine life in particular should we be imbued with? What direction should we take? Which pathway should we follow? What is our vocation, our specific vocation in this century? It is to make God triumph in our midst.

And all the rest? Where else do we find God? We find God in so many things! What should we do? We should use all these means so that God may triumph in our midst.

In doing so, we will accomplish one of the greatest things the Gospel highlights for us, and what Jesus truly wants, which is to give the clearest and most unmistakable witness of his presence, which is best expressed wherever people live in unity with one another. It is the best way to bring God to the world.

So, what is the Order of Mary,[44] which is one of the parts of our Movement that God founded on earth? It is an Order not made of contemplatives, nor scholars, not any of the other things I mentioned before. It is an Order in which the members, being united with each other, are full of God, because they have drawn God from various sources, such as the hierarchy, the Gospel,

---

44. For a few years after 1950, it was thought that the Work of Mary consisted of three parts: the "Order of Mary" made of the focolarini, the "League" for the men and women religious and priests, and a wider movement for the laity.

the Eucharist. . . . Thus, filled with God, they unite and make Jesus triumph in their midst. And they will offer the world such a spectacle that everyone in the world will say: "*These* are the disciples of Christ." They will say: "I believe in the Church because I have seen you. I believe in God, I have seen God, because I have seen you."

This is the vocation of the Order of Mary.

Therefore, considering it well, looking at it from God's point of view, we perceive that it is a divine vocation. It is a vocation that requires us to give all that we have. We have to leave everything spiritually, and also concretely. We have to leave father, mother, wife, children, fields, even our own way of thinking. We have to give up everything, and like pieces of wood in the fire, allow Jesus in our midst to consume us. That's when we will truly be the "salt of the earth," which is what God asks from us in this day and age. We will be the "light of the world."

Jesus in the midst and the Mariapolis (City of Mary)

Jesus in the midst should be the characteristic of every aspect of the life of the Movement, in all its various branches and activities. This is particularly true for the temporary and permanent Mariapolises, where people of various vocations, ages, and social categories gather together in what resembles a "little town," either for a few days during the summer or on a yearlong basis. Both aim to be a foretaste of the eschatological presence of God in the heavenly Jerusalem.

From a talk to the residents of Loppiano
Loppiano, Italy, March 28, 1972

The "Mariapolis" teaches you how to bring about a continuous resurrection of Christ among all of you, of Christ living among you.

This, I would say, is the specific vocation of the Mariapolis. It is the whole reason God gave birth to this little town. It is meant to be a foretaste of the heavenly Jerusalem, as is written: "I saw the holy city, the new Jerusalem, coming down out of heaven from God, prepared as a bride adorned for her husband. And I heard a loud voice from the throne saying, "See, the home of God is among mortals. He will dwell with them. They will be his people, and God himself will be with them" (Rv 21:2-4).

You can never be without God, without Jesus spiritually present in your midst. If he is not present, or if his presence has faded, the vocation of the Mariapolis is undermined.

Jesus in the midst is the life of the focolare households

In a special way, Jesus in the midst characterizes the life of the focolare household, where people who have consecrated their life to God live together and take the commitment to keep him present among them 24 hours a day. In the draft of one of the first Statutes of the new Movement, it was already clear that his presence was fundamental, making the focolare comparable to a church.

From one of her writings
1951

The focolare has to be a church, a temple, the temple of the living God, not because of religious pictures (that should be there, but like in any normal family), but because of the continual, warm, silent, constructive, fruitful, luminous presence of God among people united in the name of Jesus.

Jesus has to live among the members of the focolare, because it is for him and in him that the Father of all these children is also present.

Without him the focolarini would be like monks without a habit

From a page of her diary
August 15, 1970

A few days ago, I was struck by the fact that on the very first page of our Rule[45] we put the phrase concerning Jesus in the midst, as the synthesis of our vocation, the norm of all other norms, which have no value if he is not there.

How then can we imagine a focolare that stays even for one minute without Jesus in the midst? The focolarini there would be like monks without a habit, without a monastery, without a rule, without a timetable, without a superior, etc.

Everything that the focolarini do without his presence is wasted, it doesn't count, it falls into nothing-

---

45. The "Rule" was formulated for the life of the focolarini at that time. Some years later the Statutes were written for the whole Work of Mary, with separate "Regulations" for the internal life of the focolarini, as well as for all the other vocations and branches.

ness, it doesn't lead to heaven, it doesn't help us progress, on the contrary!

Jesus in the midst is everything for us!

Our relationships need to be transparent, like in the Trinity

In the following letter, Chiara speaks of the focolare as a family, and since it is God's will for us, the bonds in this family have to be greater than those of our natural families. Therefore, in order to overcome our trials, it is important to share everything, including any difficulties we might experience.

From a letter to the focolarini
Rocca di Papa, Italy, September 23, 1969

So that our community might be a true focolare, as God has conceived it, everything has to be open and transparent, while remaining within the intimacy of our family, just as everything is transparent in the Trinity and yet enclosed within the unity of the one God. We shape our lives on the life of the Trinity, and just as in the Trinity, unity is generated by the fact that the divine Persons are love for one another, so we need to understand that a focolare cannot be called such if the focolarini are not love for one another. . . .

We know that within a family the parents have great love and care for their children, helping them during all the difficult stages in their life, doing everything for them and keeping faith in them. In the same way, and even more so, we have to await the time when we can help one another to become saints together. How can this happen? By communicating what is in our soul, as a gift of love to the others. It doesn't matter whether what we say sounds to us like progress or a setback. It is only with Jesus in the midst that it's possible to see clearly what it is.

The focolarini are never alone

From a page of her diary
July 23, 1980

The norm of norms is the presence of Jesus in the community. . . . Therefore, the focolarini are never alone. They have, according to their Statutes, Jesus among them. What more do we want? I understand why, even though they are scattered all over the world and live in very diverse environments, they give the impression of being protected. We can be sure of them, as if they were covered in armor and possess the power to go ahead, because their home is Jesus, Jesus is the atmosphere they breathe, Jesus is what they have and what they give.

I think that since we will soon have Jesus in the Eucharist in our focolare houses, I feel (this is my impression) that since we have made the effort to have him spiritually present in our midst, this is his response, an example of "it will be given to you" (see Lk 6:38).

Jesus in the midst is everything for the focolare, its supreme ornament. And our houses (as a replica of the little house of Nazareth) contain him, like when he was a little child in the Holy Land.

2. The Path to Collective Holiness: The Exterior Castle

The way to sanctity for the members of the Work of Mary is a new, communitarian path, and to describe it Chiara coined the expression, the "exterior castle." It is a reference to the "interior castle" of Saint Teresa of Avila, while expressing the novelty of the communitarian experience lived in the focolare. The exterior castle, Chiara said, is the kingdom of God among us, brought about by the presence of Christ among two or more persons united in his name. It has both communitarian and individual dimensions.

A wonderful plan of God

The first time the expression "exterior castle" occurs is in one of Chiara's writings during the well-known period of light, called Paradise '49.[46] We quote a very brief and succinct passage of it here, together with a footnote Chiara added at a later date.

From one of her writings
November 8, 1950

God's design is marvelous: this Kingdom of heaven, this exterior castle where God is among us.

Note added to the text years later:
Here . . . already there appears the idea of the exterior castle, prefiguring the reality of the Movement,

---

46. This refers to a period of mystical experience lived as a group, which started on July 16, 1949, with the pact of unity between Chiara Lubich and Igino Giordani and which lasted for almost two years.

where Christ is present and gives light to all its parts. Probably at that time I already knew something of Saint Teresa of Avila's teaching about the interior castle, but here I do not mean to make any comparison.

Jesus makes light shine from every part of the Movement

In response to a question about the meaning of the expression "exterior castle," Chiara recalled that she had already spoken of this image in the Mariapolis of 1959, when she was describing Jesus in the midst.

From an answer to the school for women focolarine
November 25, 1961

Can you explain to me what the "exterior castle" is and how it can be implemented throughout the whole Work of Mary?

By exterior castle we mean that the characteristic of our vocation is putting Jesus in our midst, unlike, for example, Saint Teresa of Avila, whose vocation is contemplation, and therefore, looking for God within oneself. We have Jesus in our midst here, just as he is present in the midst of the whole Movement. He is the one who governs us all. He is always the same Jesus. . . . Jesus is present in every part of the Movement and in the whole of it.

We will reach holiness if we travel together towards God in unity, which means that we do not reach holiness individually; we reach holiness only together, because God has called us precisely to unity! If we achieve unity, we will, as a consequence, become holy.

In the Mariapolis of 1959, in the talk given by Natalia[47] about Jesus in the midst, the Work of Mary was already viewed in this way. It was said that the whole Movement could be considered as an exterior castle, in which Jesus—the king—lives, illuminating all the various parts of the Movement. Therefore, we said that the many windows of the castle could be opened and the light would shine out.

Maybe a little tower of the castle would represent your focolare and if its window were opened, you should see the light coming from it, which is Jesus in your midst.

Walking along a collective way to holiness

From a worldwide conference call
Loppiano, Italy, May 14, 1987

For us it is God's will to walk along the path of collective sanctity. And in order to do this we need to be aware of two aspects of our spirituality that are absolutely essential. We cannot become saints unless we keep the risen Lord alive in us and among us.

We live in the midst of the world and, wherever we turn, we encounter something that is in opposition to Christ and his mentality. In the world, we breathe the air of consumerism, hedonism, materialism and secularism.

How can we constantly, and more effectively, bring the presence of God into modern society?

---

47. Chiara's first companion. The talks on the points of the spirituality during the Mariapolis of 1959 were all prepared by Chiara Lubich but given by various of her first companions.

How can we defend ourselves from the snares of the world that are always ready to attack and discourage us? How can we keep the resolutions we make during moments of grace?

Mary has given us a fabulous opportunity with her Movement. She has formed everywhere, and in different ways, many small and large communities that have as their vocation keeping Jesus present in their midst. Therefore, she asks us not only to overcome our own personal difficulties by embracing Jesus forsaken, so that the risen Lord may live in us, but also to establish unity with our brothers and sisters, so that the risen Lord may be in our midst.

She knows that, in a world like ours, it would be very hard for us to make it on our own. That's why she "invented" a spirituality that is collective, lived by a number of people together. We can all testify that this is a real necessity.

I remember that in the beginning of the Movement, when we first discovered the existence of Jesus in the midst, we realized what an enormous contribution he brought to our spiritual life. Before that, we experienced how weak we were, how unable to carry out our resolutions, how often we doubted the choices we had made for God. We didn't understand how to live the Gospel. And the same thing can happen now.

When is it that we are again attracted by the world and its proposals? When do we easily give up the struggle that we have to wage every day to be Christians and members of our Movement? When do doubts arise more easily about our vocation?

These things happen when the presence of Jesus in the midst diminishes, when we live alone (separated from the others). And this makes sense, because Scripture says: "Woe to the one who is alone . . ." (Ecclus. 4:10), whereas: "A brother helped by a brother is like a strong city."[48]

And as John Chrysostom wonderfully explains: "the strength that comes from being united is great . . . because, being united together, charity grows; and, if charity grows, then the reality of God will necessarily grow [among us]."[49] Therefore, God is the strength that springs from unity. It is Jesus in our midst.

So that we, who follow the path of unity, can successfully reach the goal of holiness, Jesus in the midst is essential. To avoid the risk of failing, we need to always renew his presence in our focolares, in our nuclei, in our units, in our meetings, in our centers, in our families. And if it is God's will that we should spread out and be alone in the world, we have to find every opportunity to establish his presence with someone else who shares our Ideal. Only in this way will we have the light, the strength, the peace and the ardor that are indispensable for our total fulfillment.

Thus, we have to achieve holiness by keeping the risen Lord alive in us, through our love for Jesus forsaken, and among us, through the same love.

This is the plan that God and Mary have for us. Only in this way will we become holy.

48. See John Chrysostom, Expos. In Ps. 133, PG 55, 385.
49. Epist. Ad Hebr. 10,25. Hom. 19,1 PG 63, 140.

3. Another Mary

The Work of Mary, as its name indicates, has a strong bond with the mother of Jesus. Like her, who gave Jesus to the world, the Work of Mary has only one task: to give Jesus back to the world, by keeping him spiritually present in the midst of people united in his name. And it was Mary who also gave life to the Movement, who conceived it as it is, and nourished it with her spiritual milk.

A Marian function

An answer to a question of a group of priests
Frascati, Italy, March 17, 1975

> *The experience of this school for priests has made us appreciate Jesus in the midst. What place does Mary have in this?*

In order to put Jesus in our midst, we repeat the role of Mary. . . . We can generate Jesus in our midst by living mutual love. Therefore, ours is a Marian role. . . . It is a Marian role to put Jesus in our midst; it means generating one of the presences of Christ.

Mary generates Jesus in the midst

From a talk to the school of formation for focolarini
Grottaferrata, Italy, February 26, 1964

Jesus in our midst is what makes our Movement the Work of Mary. I would like to make this very clear, so that there are no misunderstandings. There are movements or institutions in the Church that are named for a saint, or for Mary, or for God, such as Opus Dei ("Work of God" in Latin). Why is ours called the "Work of Mary"? Was it because we wanted to give a title to Mary; was it because Mary keeps everyone under her mantle; was it because . . . ? No, it was not for any of those reasons. It was because when Mary lived on earth her task was not, for example, to found a religious order, or establish a convent. She gave life to Jesus.

Mary, who lives in the Work of Mary, generates Jesus in the midst, and therefore, keeping Jesus in our midst makes us become Mary. He is Mary's masterpiece, or better, the fruit of the Work of Mary is that it makes us become Mary, another Mary.

Now, when we give Jesus to the world spiritually, with all the methods he suggested to us in the Rule that imbues our life, since he is the one who regulates our life, who supports us, and is everything for us, when we give Jesus, we have done everything. Now, if Jesus then converts people, if Jesus does this or that, if Jesus brings unity to the right and to the left, that's his business. Our duty is to give him to the world.

This is the heritage I leave to you

From a page of her diary
Barcelona, Spain, December 1, 2002

Thinking back to our recent General Assembly, I recalled that I said I would leave all of you, as my inheritance, Jesus in the midst. Today, with amazement, I saw that heritage with new eyes.

I understood that if, upon my death, I would leave the whole world to each of you, there would be absolutely no comparison. *Jesus* is the supreme good and everyone can inherit it. Why is that? Because he is nothing less than the result of putting our spirituality into practice. Living one fundamental point after the other, we will manage to offer Jesus to the world. And perhaps that's why we can say: "In the Church, my mother, I will be Mary." Mary, overshadowed by the Holy Spirit, offered him physically to the world. Because of the light of a charism [of the Holy Spirit], we can offer him spiritually.

From an answer to the focolarini in Spain
Madrid, Spain, December 5, 2002

> *In recent months, there have been two important events—the letter from the pope about the rosary and the ecumenical meetings in Geneva. How do you see these events? Do you see a connection between them?*

These events brought back into focus our true vocation of being another Mary. But what kind of Mary? . . . The one revealed to us by our charism. As you know, I saw her to be all and only "word of God" and also the Mother of God. . . .

Another discovery I made during recent trips was that our whole spirituality, in all its aspects—God-love, the will of God, Jesus forsaken—all serves to generate Christ in our midst.

This is the inheritance I would like to leave behind when I die. Like mothers, who leave a will, giving their children their inheritance, no matter how small or big it might be, I want to leave you Jesus in the midst. Because of the charism God has given me, I have been so very blessed that now I can tell you: "You know how to keep Jesus in the midst. This is the heritage I will leave you, which means I am leaving you Jesus Christ, the means to become Mary." . . .

Our Movement and our whole spirituality, right up to our most recent discoveries, are the "milk" of Mary, they are Marian spirituality. What is the outcome? Jesus in the midst, to bring Jesus in the midst to the world, everywhere.

To be radical in living our charism

Reading a book about Mother Teresa of Calcutta, in which her radical love for the poor is evident, Chiara was reminded of the specific charism that God has given to the Work of Mary: to be another little Mary, who offers Jesus to the world. In the light of this rediscovery, Chiara proposed to radically renew her own life in the focolare in order to be consistent with the charism.

From a worldwide conference call
Castel Gandolfo, Italy, February 20, 2003

Each charism is like a wonderful, unique, original flower, different from all the others. This was also the opinion of Mother Teresa. Whenever we met, she would always tell me: "What I am doing, you cannot do. What you are doing, I cannot do."

Prompted by this conviction, I began to read our Statutes, convinced that I would find there the measure and type of radicalness that the Lord is asking of me.

I opened it and immediately, on the very first page, I had a small spiritual shock, as when you discover something in that very moment, and yet I have known this for almost sixty years! It was the "norm of norms, the premise of every other rule" in my life, in our life, which is to "generate"—as Pope Paul VI expressed it—and to maintain, first and foremost, the presence of Jesus among us through our mutual love. We need to do this even while carrying out large events, or during quite exceptional encounters, or when achieving great gains for the kingdom of God.

I understood at once that this is my, our, most important task, especially today. We have to be a little Mary in the Church, "a presence of Mary on earth, almost a continuation of her,"[50] both individually and with the entire Work of Mary. We have to be another Mary who offers Jesus to the world.

I immediately made the resolution to live this norm, first of all in my focolare, and with all those around me.

We know that Jesus said: "Let anyone among you who is without sin be the first to throw a stone at her" (Jn 8:7). Not everything is perfect in our focolare either: an unnecessary word said by me or by others, too much silence, a rash judgment, a small attachment, a suffering not borne patiently, all of which undoubtedly makes Jesus feel uncomfortable among us, if it doesn't prevent his presence altogether.

I understood that I had to be the first to make room for him, to smooth out everything, to fill in all the empty spots, seasoning everything with the greatest charity, putting up with everything in the others and in myself. "Bearing" or "putting up with others" are words we don't generally use, but the Apostle Paul advises us to do just that (see 1 Cor 13:7).

---

50. *General Statutes*, Art. 2.

Certainly, "to put up with others" requires not just an ordinary kind of charity. It is a special charity, the quintessence of charity.

I began to do it. And there are positive results!

On other occasions, I would have immediately invited my companions to do the same. Not this time. I feel that I have to be the first to do all my part, and it's working. Besides, it fills my heart with happiness, perhaps because, in this way, he comes back into our midst and remains.

Later on, I will tell them, but I will continue to feel the duty to go forward as if I were alone in this endeavor.

And my greatest joy is when I think of Jesus' words: "I desire mercy, not sacrifice" (Mt 9:13). Mercy! This is the refined charity that is asked of us and which is worth more than sacrifice, because the most beautiful sacrifice is love capable even of bearing with everything, capable of forgiving and forgetting when necessary.

To be little Marys, to ensure the presence of Jesus in the world, we need to live the "premise of every other rule," which is constant mutual charity that blossoms into mercy.

This is the radical nature of our life. This is the total commitment we are asked to live.

4. Founder, Legislator, Guide

Each order or religious family in the Church, Chiara explains, is like the incarnation of one word of the Gospel, and the various founders were the personifica-

tion of that word.[51] *The "word" of the Work of Mary, Chiara continues, is, "That they may all be one" and the true founder is not an individual person, but Jesus in the midst of people united in his name. In saying this, she does not deny her own part as a particular instrument of God, but points out that God had prepared her and given her the idea, but he had also prepared other people who were so empty of themselves that they were able to take in this new idea. Thus, the spirituality of unity came to life from the very beginning as something generated by Jesus in the midst. He is the one who sustained everything, especially in difficult times, and who guided every step, opening up unimaginable paths. He was also the one who suggested the guidelines of our life that were later inserted in the Statutes, which states that the premise of every other rule is mutual and constant love that brings about the presence of Jesus in the midst. It is this "norm of norms" that will guarantee that the Movement will continue in the future according to the plan of God.*

He drew up guidelines full of light

From a talk prepared for the Mariapolis
1959

The Work of Mary is a magnificent work in the Church, for which God formulated very precise guidelines. But who made us understand them? It wasn't human intelligence, or mere human reasoning. It was Jesus in our midst who helped us, who showed us where God wanted us to be, who mapped out a path for us, and not just for us, but for everyone.

---

51. See Chiara Lubich, *The Church*, eds. Brendan Leahy and Hubertus Blaumeiser (New York: New City Press, 2018), 49.

Who was it that throughout the history of the Movement devised the guidelines so full of light for its organization? Who, if not Jesus in the midst, gave rise to the various vocations? Every vocation is divine, just as every vocation implements the same Ideal.

He is the one behind the norms we live by, behind every step we take.

And when we do not know how to go ahead, to whom do we turn if not to him, telling one another: "Let's put Jesus in the midst so that we can understand the will of God." He alone is the light of our lives, the solution to all our problems.

He is our leader

If someone were to ask what the presence of Jesus in the midst in the Movement means to us, we should say that Jesus in the midst is the founder and legislator of the Movement. . . . And since the [Catholic] Church has approved it, we owe it to the fact that the same Christ lives in it as lives in the hierarchy.

Jesus in our midst is our leader in every front the Movement works on. Some of these fronts are well known and need to be preserved and expanded. Others were not yet known, but Jesus pointed them out to us from time to time, and often they are things we never expected to be involved in. For it is in God and only in him that the plan of the Work of Mary is drawn up, and it is Jesus in our midst who gradually clarifies the various steps of this plan.

Jesus in the midst is the superior of every small or large community

To the school of formation for the women focolarine
Grottaferrata, Italy, February 26, 1964

You know that our Rule requires that we have superiors. . . . Now this superior, who has been given to us by the Church, has the task of ensuring that the Rule is observed. In the Rule, it is said that the rule of rules, the norm of every norm, the premise of every other rule is Jesus in the midst. Who governs you? Jesus. The other (the superior) is an instrument who speaks. So the true superior of the Movement has to be Jesus in the midst, and if he is not, it is no longer the Work of Mary.

Put Jesus in the midst and do whatever you want

Authority must be a service, a gift. Chiara explains how this is possible by having Jesus in the midst before everything else, and how this gives equilibrium to the life of the focolarini.

From an answer at a school for those responsible for the focolare
March 28, 1986

How can we reconcile authority with service?

How to reconcile it? Well, we don't reconcile it. For us, there is no authority that is not a gift, that is not a service. . . . We have to put mutual love above everything else. Mutual love has to be the basis for every use of authority. . . .

If you first put into practice mutual love, then whatever you tell the others will be easily accepted, because if there is mutual love, the person responsible for the focolare expresses the wishes of Jesus in the midst, and so the focolarini feel that what they are told to do is truly God's will. Besides, if there is mutual love, the focolarino is ready to give his life for you, and if he is ready to give his life for you, he is also ready to obey the small thing that you ask him to do. But if there is no Jesus in the midst, the slightest thing can upset him. Therefore, we go ahead with a certain equilibrium. . . . We know that our rule is to always put Jesus in the midst, and then you can do whatever you want. Saint Augustine said, "Love and do whatever you want." But I would say, "Put Jesus in the midst and do whatever you want."

Jesus in the midst will save the Movement

On several occasions, Chiara was asked how we can be faithful to the charism in the future and ensure that Jesus in the midst will always prevail and not someone's partial interpretation of the charism.

From an answer to a group of men religious of the Movement
Saint Maurice, Switzerland, July 29, 1987

> *Recently, there is the growing awareness among us that we cannot only live the Ideal ourselves but have to pass it on to others. Do you feel that the new generations have the grace to make the Movement grow and develop in the future, so that life will continue with the same fidelity to the charism as always?*

I am often asked this question, and I ask myself the same thing. My confidence in the future lies in our Statutes. The premise for all the rules it contains . . . is Jesus in the midst, that is, all that we do, all that we propose to improve, etc., is worth nothing, if we do not first have Jesus in our midst. Before all else, there must be Jesus in the midst in the Movement.

There was a priest from Czechoslovakia, a saint, who once told me: "This Rule of ours is certainly quite extraordinary because it's based on a mystical principle." And he wasn't wrong, because nothing has value for us if there is not Jesus in the midst.

So my trust lies in him. And I remember, when we were still young, we used to say: "Oh, my God, we have only been living the Ideal for three years—or we have only been living the Ideal for five years—how can we presume to conquer the world?" We *believed* we could reach "that they may all be one," which was our goal, because we trusted totally in him. Yes, we said, it's true that I'm like this, and he is like that, but we have Jesus in our midst, and he is the one who will conquer the world—*he* will do it!

So if in the future those in the Movement continue to be faithful to living the Statutes, they will be faithful to Jesus in the midst and so he will be the one to make the Movement go ahead. It will not be the new president, or the new council . . . or a new center of the branch of the men religious who [will] carry it forward, but it will be him here and there, him everywhere. This is what I believe and it is faith based on my experience, because even in the past I did not trust in myself nor in others. We kept putting our trust in him and he gave us the light and led us forward. He brought us where we are now. So there is a good basis for what I am telling you.

From an answer to the school of formation for focolarini
Loppiano, Italy, May 15, 1987

> *In the future, when you will no longer be with us physically, how can we ensure that Jesus in the midst will always prevail and not our own ideas, our own way of seeing things, or one of the branches of the Movement, or something else partial and relative, instead of the whole Work of Mary in unity?*

My confidence for the future lies precisely with Jesus in the midst. . . . A thousand different interpretations of the Movement may well emerge, and I have already heard a few in some places. But Jesus in the midst will be the one who saves the unity of the Movement and who will also save the different interpretations, in the sense that he will help you to interpret everything in exactly the same way.

This is because we count, precisely, on a mystical factor in our life, which is the presence of Christ in our midst. . . . My trust—keep this in mind—is Jesus in the midst, because if there is Jesus in the midst you won't swerve off the path, you won't interpret things in the wrong way, you will interpret everything correctly.

Chapter V

Jesus in the Midst and the Church

"Small Churches Everywhere"

The presence of Jesus in the midst in the focolare made Chiara and her companions feel like true children of the Church. "The Lord helped us rediscover the mystery of the Church"—she told a group of focolarini in 1971—"that is, he made us understand what it means to be *Church and how to live that reality with greater awareness. He 'dusted off' a spirituality which is the spirituality of the Mystical Body, the spirituality of the Church." This was clear to them from the very beginning of their new life, which began, as she herself recalled, in the same year that the encyclical* Mystici Corporis *(On the Mystical Body of Christ)* was promulgated by Pope Pius XII. *The charism of unity that God was bestowing on the whole Church was nothing other than a "divine injection" so that the Mystical Body would live the dynamics of love already written in its DNA.*[52] *Jesus in the midst was the Jesus of the Church-as-communion, who made sure that even the smallest cell of it, inserted as a branch on the vine, was "Church," "Church in substance," pulsating with the divine life he shared with us.*

When the Movement first began, and in the years that followed, the novelty of Jesus in the midst was so much in evidence precisely because it was lived in very concrete ways. The "network of dark tunnels" that unite the mem-

---

52. See Lubich, *The Church*, 51, 52, and 106.

bers of the Body of Christ were being illuminated by the life of mutual love in which Christ manifested himself.[53]

As Chiara explained several times, this does not mean that Christ was not present in the Church as the risen Lord, or that he is not present now. However, his presence in the midst was not highlighted in the past and is not always so evident now. Sometimes it looks more like a "pale light" that is almost dying out. Because of the charism that God had given her, she felt called to ensure that Jesus in the midst shone brightly everywhere. In this way, he would be able to achieve his goal, which is the unity of the whole Church.

The relationship between Jesus in the midst and the presence of the risen Christ in the Church, and also in the whole cosmos, was further explained and explored in the years that followed, with the help of the theologians of the Abba School[54], as we will see below in the second section of this chapter.

The ecumenical influence of Jesus in the midst has proved to be of particular significance for our times. He is the "strong point" of ecumenism, which binds together the members of various Churches and ecclesial communities in a fraternity in God that makes them be "Church" together. Even though it is not yet possible to share the same Eucharist together, we can prepare the ground with Jesus in our midst, waiting for the time when there will be full and visible communion among all Christians.

---

53. Lubich, *Meditations,* 38.

54. Starting from the early 90s, the Abba School has studied the doctrine that emerges from the charism of unity and especially from the writings of the mystical experience of 1949 and 1950 (Paradise '49).

1. Jesus in the Midst Makes Us "Church"

The Church defines itself as the Body of Christ (see 1 Cor 12:12-27) and Jesus in the midst is therefore her lifeblood, by which "living cells" are being formed. The documents of the Second Vatican Council, together with theological reflections that followed it, brought into evidence the fact that the universal Church is present in every local church, if it is united to the whole body. Thus, the Church is a reflection of the life of the Trinity, which is one and three. In full harmony with this dynamism and in accordance with the teachings of the Fathers of the Church, Chiara affirmed that the Church is reflected and present in every small part of it, "where two or three are gathered" in the name of Jesus. In this perspective, we recall that Jesus in the midst brings with him his Spirit, the Holy Spirit, who is defined by the Fathers as "the soul of the Church."

Living cells

In a well-known text, published in 1949 under the title "The Resurrection of Rome," Chiara explains how, by "resurrecting" Christ in our neighbor by loving them, we can then live mutual love and compose together a "living cell" of the Mystical Body. Thus Christ will live in each one and also in their midst. However, the goal is always to vivify the whole body, as we find explained in a text by Chiara a few days later. The footnotes were inserted into the text by Chiara herself in subsequent years.

Some excerpts of her writings
October 1949

Resurrecting there Jesus, another Christ, another God-who-is-human, the manifestation of the Father's goodness here below, the Eye of God upon humanity. Thus, I extend the Christ in me to my brother or sister and I form a living and complete cell of the Mystical Body of Christ,[55] a living cell, a hearth of God,[56] that holds the Fire to be communicated and with that the Light.

It is God who makes two into one, placing himself third, as their relationship: Jesus among us.

Thus, love circulates and like a blazing river carries naturally (through the law of communion that is in-nate in it) every other thing that the two possess so that they put in common their goods, those of the spirit and those that are material.

And this is an effective and outward witness to a unitive love, the true love, that of the Trinity.

Then truly the whole Christ lives again in both and each one and among us.

November 1949

We must create continually these living cells of the Mystical Body of Christ—which are brothers and sisters united in his name—to give life to the whole Body.

---

55. It is like this because, according to his promise, it really is him in that cell: "Where two or three are gathered in my name, I am there among them" (Mt 18:20).

56. That is, all fire, which is the fusion into one, into a single Jesus, of all that we are and all that we have.

Although only a few, we are Church

Chiara found great joy in finding that the Fathers of the Church, the Council documents, and some theologians confirmed what she had experienced regarding the ecclesial dimension of "where two or more are gathered. . ."

We have always liked the statement of Tertullian: "Where three (are gathered), even if they are lay people, there is the Church."[57] Yes, because we are often just a small group united and inserted juridically into the entire Church of Christ. Therefore, even if there are only a few of us, we are "Church," "living Church," because of the presence of Jesus among us.

And John of Cyprus says: "What is the Church of God . . . ? It is the sacred encounter in the name of the true Light that illuminates every person who comes into the world. It is an encounter that is born and grows not only where there are numerous people who are happy and successful, but also among those of humble origins. In fact, in one passage the Word said, 'Where two or three are gathered in my name, I am there among them.'"[58]

The Second Vatican Council and the pope have repeatedly stressed that any community united as one family in the name of the Lord rejoices in his presence. It is this kind of fraternity that makes us Church, as Odo Casel affirms: "It is not that the one *Ecclesia* [Church] shatters into a plurality of individual communities, nor that the multiplicity of the individual communities united together forms the one *Ecclesia*. The *Ecclesia* is only one, wherever it appears; it is whole and

---

57. Tertullian, *De exhort. Cast. 7,* PL2, 971.
58. John of Cyprus, *Palamiticarum transgressionum liber,* PG 152, 702.

undivided, even where only two or three are gathered in the name of Christ."[59] Perhaps we Christians are not aware of what an extraordinary opportunity we have.

Go through life as a small church

We have to make ourselves one with our neighbor . . . to the point of establishing between us the essential elements needed for the Lord to say of us: "Where two or three are gathered in my name, I am there among them." We have to reach the point of guaranteeing, as much as we can, the presence of Jesus and then to go through life, always, as a small church, being "Church" even when we are at home, at school, in the workshop, in parliament.

We will go through life like the disciples of Emmaus, with that third Person among us who gives divine value to all our actions. Then it will no longer be ourselves who act in life, as wretched and limited, alone and afflicted as we are. The Almighty will journey with us. And those who are united to him bear great fruit. We will increase from one cell to many cells, forming always new tissue.[60]

Invade humanity with small churches composed of two or more

The possibility of "being church," even where there are no churches made of stone, gave birth to Chiara's passion of invading humanity with an infinite number of churches, formed by people who have Jesus in their midst.

---

59. Odo Casel, *Il mistero dell'ecclesia (The Mystery of the Church)*, Rome, 1965, 181.

60. Lubich, *Meditations*, 86-88.

Remember this: none of us needs anything exteriorly in order to offer Jesus to modern society. There is no need for freedom of the press, no need for sermons, no need for churches made of bricks. Nothing is necessary, if God takes all of those things away from us, when we have nothing exteriorly.

There is a presence of Jesus that is possible to have in every country, in every environment. It is a presence that has come into evidence in a particular way in our times, after the Second Vatican Council and also with our Movement. It is the presence of Christ that God promises to us wherever there are two or more united in his name.

From a talk with the residents of Loppiano
Loppiano, Italy, November 27, 1975

What struck me most, perhaps, in looking more into the reality of his presence, was that for him just a few things are enough. All that is needed is two or three people, and wherever he is, he creates what he came on earth to bring us: the Church. And so he aroused within me an immense passion to build thousands and thousands of churches, hundreds of thousands, millions, really millions of churches, made not of stone, but of two or three people united in his name scattered throughout the world. . . .

The idea of being able to build, with Jesus in person in our midst, an infinite number of churches, is the idea that I find so exhilarating in these days. I would like to communicate it to all of you, to tell you that we have a treasure in our hands, which people who come here for the first time aren't able to understand.

But you, because you have been chosen, and you are young, and you are either small or you have learned this spirit as children, you know what it means. You know because Jesus in the midst has accompanied you up to now; Jesus in the midst has brought you ahead; he has given you light; he has dried your tears; he has taken away your sufferings, your anguish, your temptations. It has been him, Jesus in the midst, who is our light.

To answer your question, I would like to make you aware of who he is, and above all, to communicate to you the passion that burns in my heart, the desire to invade humanity by building all these churches throughout the whole world.

The Holy Spirit, the soul of the Church

It is impossible to separate the action of the risen Lord from that of the Holy Spirit. Each one contains the other, each one implies the other. This also applies to the work of God in every single person. In the gifts of light and peace that Jesus in the midst brings to us, we recognize the gifts of the Holy Spirit. It is the same with regard to the life of the Church. The Holy Spirit is called "the soul of the Church," and through him, since we are baptized in one Spirit, we form one body, the Body of Christ (see 1 Cor 12:13).

When we live in unity, the presence of Jesus "is felt, seen, enjoyed. . . . Everyone enjoys his presence, everyone suffers from his absence. It is peace, joy, love, ardor, a climate of heroism, of supreme generosity." And these effects, this atmosphere are the fruit of the spirit of Jesus, who is the Holy Spirit himself. The spirit of the risen Jesus in our midst makes us Jesus, and others also see us as the continuation of him, as the Body of Christ, the Church.[61]

2. Called to Bring Him to Life

As mentioned before, towards the end of her life, and with the help of several theologians, Chiara presented a new synthesis of the ecclesiological dimension of the presence of Jesus in the midst. She inserted it into the global presence of the risen Christ within the universe and clarified in greater detail both the continuous presence of Christ in the Church and the specific task of those called to live the charism of unity.

We find this in two themes she prepared for the bishop-friends of the Movement—the first one for Catholic bishops in August 2004, and the second one for bishops of various Churches a few months later. The latter, because of her illness, was presented and read by Emmaus, Maria Voce, a focolarina who, a few years later was elected President of the Movement after Chiara's death. We present some of the main points that summarize these talks. The subtitles were added by the editor.

November 2004

---

61. Chiara Lubich, *Jesus: The Heart of His Message* (New York: New City Press, 1997), 27.

The Christ of the resurrection

The early Church was convinced of the presence of Jesus in the midst from the very beginning, as the writings of the New Testament testify. The Gospels were written with the certainty that Jesus, precisely because he is risen, continues to act and speak within the Christian community today. He does so through his words and actions, which are preserved in the Gospels.

In fact, the Gospels are not just a biography to help us remember Jesus, but rather an invitation to meet him and follow him in the here and now, because he is truly present today, even if we do not see him. This is what we have always experienced in living the charism of unity, because we have seen, for example, that the promises of Jesus are being fulfilled even today.

It is because of his resurrection that Jesus is still present with us. And we feel his presence when we experience the fullness of life.

After the resurrection, Jesus is totally different. His relationship with the cosmos changed radically, so much so that he is no longer contained within time and space, as we know them. Instead, he is the one who contains within himself space and time; the physical universe and all of humanity is within him. Jesus is no longer subject to the laws that govern the world; rather, he totally dominates them.

A presence that brings together and creates communion

The risen Jesus is not a static presence. The basic characteristic of his presence consists in a unifying and therefore active principle: love.

After the resurrection, Jesus is the Christ in his total gift of love to God and to humanity. In particular, the cry of abandonment reveals that the Son fully and totally assumed the finite, sinful condition of humankind, and healed it within himself; he filled it with love.

His is, therefore, a presence that brings together and creates communion among people, and makes them one in God.

The Church: the body of the risen Christ

Jesus crucified and risen certainly reconciles all things, even to the ends of the earth. However, the universal presence of the risen Lord occurs first and foremost within the Church; it becomes actual and visible within the Church. . . . The Church has a very privileged relationship with the Lord. The risen Jesus is the head of both the cosmos and the Church, but only the Church is his body.

The most profound identity of every real community, of every individual community and not only of the universal Church, is the person of the risen Jesus himself, as Paul wrote in his letter to the Corinthians: "You are the body of Christ" (1 Cor 12:27).

The community *is* Jesus present. However—pay attention!—this is true and is visible only if Christians love one another, if they live in love.

The presence of Christ in the Church is always a call to unity, a call to bring to life the body of Christ by living mutual love. It is the call to unity that the charism of the Movement engraved on our souls. . . .

All throughout history, therefore, Jesus continues to bring the Church together into one, inserting into his body those who are baptized. The community, therefore, finds its true identity in something that precedes it: the presence of the risen Christ. He is the one who brings together and unites believers with himself and with each other. . . .

The presence of the risen Jesus, however, awaits—I repeat—something else. It requires our response. Only if we love, can we ensure that the presence of Jesus becomes a reality in our lives.

The vocation of the Church, as of each individual, is a vocation to live in unity, a unity that is concretely implemented. As Paul says, "the only thing that counts is faith working through love" (Gal 5:6).

Jesus in the midst: the spirituality of the Church

Throughout the centuries, the presence of Christ, who constitutes the very soul of the Church and of every Christian community, has never been lacking. He continues to reveal himself in every member of the body of Christ who consistently lives the faith. This is true for every religious congregation (in monasteries, convents, etc.), for every liturgical assembly, for every truly Christian family—only and always if they live in mutual love.

What is new is the need to bring this presence to its final goal, that is, to reach the unity of the whole body, and this is clearly related to our vocation to unity.

This being so, it is clear that *agape* [divine love] is primarily geared not to charitable works, but to reciprocity, to communion, which makes the Lord "visible."

Every division in the community is therefore "against its very nature" because it distorts the essence of the community, which is Christ present. Christ cannot be divided. A fragmented Christ is unrecognizable, disfigured. That is why at times people do not love the Church, because what they see—we can say—is almost a caricature of the Church.

To live intentionally with Jesus in the midst is a spirituality of the Church that makes us be "Church." In fact, Jesus in the midst is essential to the Church and not only a certain aspect of Christian life such as poverty, prayer, study, love for the marginalized, etc.

To live with Jesus in the midst means to revitalize the Church itself in its true identity and vocation.

To live with Jesus in the midst is to implement the "already" of God's plan for humanity, while working for the "yet to come."

The originality of our charism does not lie only in being aware of this truth. The charism has been given to us so that we can contribute to fulfilling the goal of "Jesus in our midst." His goal is that all Christians may live in unity.

3. An Ecclesiology of Communion

In Novo Millennio Ineunte (At the Beginning of the New Millennium) *and in his subsequent catechesis, John Paul II called for a spirituality of communion as the way to renew the Church. "To make the Church the home and school of communion: that is the great challenge facing us in the millennium which is now beginning, if we wish to be faithful to God's plan and respond to the world's deepest yearnings" (*Novo Millennio Ineunte, 43)*. The popes who came after him also echoed the need for this commitment. It had been one of the* *great innovations of the Second Vatican Council, and still remains to be fully implemented.*

The concept of Christ among his people had been dear to the Fathers of the Church, but forgotten for many centuries, during which an ecclesiology developed in which the institutional and juridical aspects were predominant. Then, under the impetus of biblical, patristic, and liturgical renewal leading up to the Second Vatican Council, the ecclesiology of communion was rediscovered in the Catholic Church. Chiara saw in this a confirmation of the direction in which the Spirit had drawn her with the gift of the charism and rejoiced at the implicit recognition of the life she had undertaken with her first companions. Since she had always been a devout daughter of the Church, she said, "It is very important to see if the charism that moves us is in harmony with the spirit of the whole Church today." Discovering this same concept in the various Council documents, she concluded: "We should pause and praise God for having guided us. . . . We can clearly see that it is Jesus in the midst who guides us, the same Jesus who presided over the Council."

From a page of her diary
Rocca di Papa, Italy, April 9, 1967

In his book, *Reaching for More,* Fr. (Pasquale) Foresi[62] speaks about Jesus in the midst and asserts: "Until the Second Vatican Council, the passage in the Gospel, 'Where two or three are gathered in my name, I am there among them,' was rarely ever mentioned. If one excludes the Council of Chalcedon (451 AD),[63] we will

---

62. Fr. Pasquale Foresi, first focolarino to become a priest; co-founder of the Movement with Chiara and Igino Giordani.

63. See PL 54: 959.

find that throughout the whole history of the Church, even in the most solemn conciliar documents, this sentence is almost never mentioned. The Second Vatican Council, however, did not produce even one document that does not underline this fundamental idea. Without a doubt, we can state that this truth was the soul of the Council, especially in its statement on collegiality. It is a sign of the times; it is a sign that the Movement was inspired by the Holy Spirit, since it is so in keeping with the direction taken by the Council."[64]

The new face of the Church

From a page of her diary
June 1967

Wherever there is Jesus in the midst, the Church is alive with the new countenance given by the (Second Vatican) Council. There is new life among the young people, in religious orders, in our Parish Movement, in our various centers and activities.

Everything is alive, full of life, really full of life. Of course, his presence is linked to a thousand aspects of unity with those in authority, with the magisterium of the Church, with the whole of humanity, and yet he brings with him the reality of something stated by the Council—the infallibility of the people of God as a whole.

Therefore, with him among us, we walk on firm ground.

Our first duty, then, is to be closely bound together and climb up the slope of the divine will, because there is no will of God for us except that expressed through people who are living in unity with all.

---

64. Pasquale Foresi, *Reaching for More* (New York: New City Press, 1974), 55.

Keep this in mind, always remember it, have this one fixed idea in your heads, and, above all, put it into practice. It is the primary, the most obvious duty of a focolarino.

To be religious today

A group of men religious priests asked Chiara if it was more important for them to concentrate on living in community with other religious so as to build the presence of Jesus in the midst or to detach themselves in order to bring God's presence into the world. Studying some documents of the Church, Chiara observes that the first call of the religious is to be like the early Christians, that is, to be a model of how the Church should be, which is, above all, a community united in Jesus.

Responding to men religious of the Movement in Poland
Lublin, Poland, June 22, 1996

You ask me: "Is it better that we go home and aim at forming a beautiful monastic life, where we all love one another and also give witness as a community? Or is it better that we go out, perhaps on our own and alone, to do apostolate in many different places?"

This dilemma could lead you astray, because it might seem that it is better to go out to other people, with courage. However, for the religious, I believe that your first call is to establish communities, that the first will of God for you is to put Jesus in the midst with the others in your monastery. Then you can start from that point and go to bring the Word of God to others.

Some religious, for example, the PIME missionaries, have as God's will for them the sentence, "Go and make disciples of all nations" (Mt 28: 19). That's fine. They adapt their charism to this requirement. However, the primary desire of God, which is recommended by the Church for the religious, is precisely that you form communities that are an example of what the Church would be if everyone lived in unity.

Our contribution to the synod

For Chiara, the Council, and in a similar way the synods of bishops, is like "the large 'focolare' of the Church from which Jesus spreads his light abundantly to illuminate the centuries to come." When she was invited to participate as an auditor at the synod of Bishops in 1999, on the topic of "Europe," she suggested to all members of the Movement how to prepare together for this event.

From a worldwide conference call
Mollens, Switzerland, August 26, 1999

I've already begun to prepare myself by reading what is called the *Instrumentum laboris*, a working document which is always prepared before such events, with the contribution of bishops from all over the world. I found these pages to be very interesting and even the title of this synod fascinated me: "Jesus Christ, alive in his Church, the source of hope for Europe." It seems to say that, if Europe can have a hope, this hope has to be based on Jesus present in his spouse, the Church.

You can easily understand that in reading these words, I spontaneously thought of that particular presence of Jesus in the community that he promised to us with the words: "For where two or three are gathered in my name, I am there among them" (Mt 18:20). This is a presence of Jesus that in no way excludes the others that we know. On the contrary! . . .

This synod is an event in the Church that all Christians should feel as their own, which they should follow, participate in, and contribute to, at least with their prayers. They say that we know how a synod begins, but we don't know how it will end. It's an event in the Church in which the Holy Spirit acts and leads us where he wills.

As you can well imagine, this event is of special interest to us. And so we ask ourselves: what attitude should we have? First of all, we should be grateful to God because certain cornerstones that are so fundamental for us in the Movement are now emerging at the level of the Church, such as, in this case, Jesus in the midst of Christians.

We should eagerly await this synod, since we know the effects of Jesus in the midst and so can almost foresee what it might produce for the spouse of Christ. Finally, we should be committed to living with greater intensity this very point, since we have been reflecting for some time now on Jesus among us.

During our last conference call, we decided to intensify our life of unity by listening more attentively to one another. So now what commitment should we make for the month of September, in order to prepare for the synod in October? What can we do for it? We can continuously renew in our hearts the solemn proposal to have Jesus present among us always, night and day, and to act accordingly. To reach this goal, when we are in contact with one or more brothers or sisters of the Ideal, we should openly and frequently declare our desire to keep Jesus in the midst. . . .

Doing this, keeping the temperature of our spiritual life high, can be our characteristic contribution to the synod.

A way of living Christianity today

If, in the past, personal union with God required that one keep a distance from other people, the spirituality of communion, as highlighted by the Council, brings about a reversal of this perspective. We find God by loving our brothers and sisters, by establishing with them the presence of Jesus in the midst. This is the exterior castle that was presented in the previous chapter.

From an answer to a group of priests and men religious of the Movement
Incisa Valdarno, Italy, May 15, 1987

How can we reconcile the desire to have a personal union with God and also unity with those who share our way of life?

The Ideal brings a real revolution in the way of living Christianity, because it places mutual and continual love before everything else, as the Gospel says: "If your brother or sister has something against you, leave your gift there before the altar and go; first be reconciled with your brother or sister" (Mt 5:23-24). What we have understood, and what everyone understands when they meet the Ideal, is that it is necessary to put mutual love at the basis of life, at the basis of our prayers, even before praying, because both Jesus and the Father tell us: "Before coming to us, be reconciled with your brother or sister. First, you have to be in unity with others." . . .

It seems from what you say that at the moment you almost consider as secondary the absence of Jesus in the midst, and you consider it much more serious that you haven't said your prayers, or didn't do some other duty, etc. However, with the passing of years, it will become such a torment for you not to have Jesus in the midst that you will no longer be able to live without him. This happens because you grow in virtue, in the principal virtue of a true Christian, who is called to live in communion with others before all else. This is what the [Second Vatican] Council repeatedly says, as well as all the synods of the bishops. "Before all else," constant and mutual love.

Allow me to tell you something. You need to make a total conversion to live the Ideal in a radical way. That's exactly what is needed. It's actually a beautiful kind of conversion because you pass from a way of life that is already good to another that is even more beautiful. It's not a conversion from evil, but it is necessary all the same. . . .

Living with Jesus in the midst, you will always be Jesus who lives, who prays for something and obtains it, who preaches and converts people, who goes to visit the sick and consoles them. If you do these things all on your own, you are still Jesus because you are in God's grace, but only in a small measure! I don't know how to explain to you how a person can be "more" Jesus or "less" Jesus. Perhaps you can understand it by considering that a saint has a greater fullness of Christ than someone else who might be filled with God only to a certain extent.

4. The Soul of Ecumenism

The ecclesial dimension of the presence of Jesus in the midst was fundamental to Chiara's experience of unity with the members of different Christian Churches and ecclesial communities, which started spontaneously in the 1960s. If we cannot yet be united in the Eucharist, we can however be united in love, in mutual love that brings about his presence, according to the promise given in Matthew 18:20. And wherever he is, there is the Church, whose essence is communion. The experience continued in the following years and was so rich and so positive that it made Chiara exclaim: "Jesus in the midst is the center-piece of our ecumenism."

We are here only to love

In a brief talk given to a group of Christians of various Churches who came to Rome to learn more about the spirit of the Movement, Chiara, perhaps for the first time, suggests the method of "the ecumenism of the people." In the years that followed, this method has borne great fruit in the development of the Movement's ecumenical relationships.

From her notes for a Focolare ecumenical meeting
Pentecost 1965

We are not here to argue about certain points (it is not a meeting of theologians), but we do need to express the truth in charity.

And our aim here is not even to pray, even though we will pray individually and all together.

We are here in order to love.

And our love should be so fervent, so purified by crucifying our ego (continuously, constantly) that those who see us can say: "These people are not Catholics, nor Lutherans, nor Anglicans, nor Orthodox: they are all *one* in Christ the Lord." . . .

Thus he will come among us spiritually, and he will see for himself how beautiful and joyful it is when brothers and sisters live together. He will guide us hour by hour, day by day, making suggestions and bringing this conference to fruition, which we have to entrust to no one else but him.

Communion with Jesus spiritually present among us

Even though full communion has not been achieved among Christians of various Churches, which would allow for full participation in the sacrament of the Eucharist, we can experience "communion" with Jesus in our midst. Maintaining mutual love so as to ensure his presence among us, we can hope that one day we will reach the crowning moment, that of receiving the Eucharist together.

At a Focolare meeting of members of the Reformed Church Rocca di Papa, Italy, May 8, 1970

The Gospel says: ". . . if you remember that your brother or sister has something against you, leave your gift there before the altar and go; first be reconciled with your brother or sister and then come and offer your gift" (Mt 5:23-24).

Now I certainly have nothing against you and I don't think you have anything against me either, but we consciously feel that we are carrying the legacy of people who have made mistakes in the past. And mistakes are never the fault of one side only.

Even if those who came before us did not reconcile with one another, we have to be reconciled among ourselves. We have to return to living in unity. So I would like to say, "Let's leave the offering for a little while at the altar and reconcile with one another." In that way we will reach full communion. . . . We need to repair this division; and the only one capable of doing that is Jesus in our midst. . . . So the only thing to do, since we cannot share the body and blood of Christ, is to receive for now Jesus spiritually present in our midst.

A light for theological dialogue

In this answer, of which we quote only a part, Chiara speaks of three forms of ecumenical dialogue in which we can participate, thanks to Jesus in the midst. They are the ecumenism of the people, that is, of life, through living mutual love; ecumenism of prayer, since "God will be more moved to act if we all pray in unity, with Jesus in our midst"; and finally, theological ecumenism.

Answer to a question during a Focolare ecumenical meeting Castel Gandolfo, Italy, April 4, 1997

The third is the theological dialogue, which will also benefit enormously from the presence of this "people" [people of various Churches living in unity]. If besides coming together, each one full of their own doctrines, the theologians on both sides meet full of love in their hearts, loving one another and establishing the presence of Jesus in their midst, Jesus certainly isn't just there doing nothing. Jesus enlightens; Jesus makes you understand; Jesus is the only truth to which everyone is tending. He will enlighten their minds; he will clarify issues so that they can understand better how to go ahead, what decisions to make, how to draw up the documents, how to understand the other person, and so on.

Dialogue of life

The Catholic bishop-friends of the Focolare, in addition to their annual meeting, also sponsor each year an ecumenical conference for bishops and leaders of various Christian Churches. The theme presented by Chiara in 2003 was on Jesus in the midst and the dialogue of life. It outlines more than forty years of the Movement's rich ecumenical experience. This excerpt speaks of one important milestone.

At an ecumenical conference of bishops
sponsored by the Focolare
Rocca di Papa, Italy, November 26, 2003

Now, after many years of ecumenical life in the Movement, we can see more clearly what our specific contribution in the ecumenical field is. It is precisely the spirituality of unity that is very useful to the cause. In fact, the lack of an ecumenical spirituality (which ecumenists today continue to underline) makes the task of building unity among the Churches much more difficult.

I became aware of what our contribution could be in London, in 1996, when I met together with many people of various Churches who all live the same life as we do, because they all belong to the Movement. I sensed that although there was not yet full communion among the Churches and ecclesial communities, we were truly a living portion of Christianity, one heart and one soul, also because of all the things that already unite us.

In fact, with all the brothers and sisters of various Churches who adhere to our Movement, in knowing one another and living together the same spirituality, which unites us and brings among us Jesus and his light, we give the utmost value to the fact that we are all members of the Mystical Body of Christ through our common baptism. We realize that we all share a common patrimony of great treasures, such as the Old and New Testaments, the dogmas of the first Councils that we shared together, the Creed (Nicene-Constantinopolitan), the Greek and Latin Church Fathers, the martyrs, and other treasures, too, such as the life of grace, and faith, hope and charity.

Before, we had not been fully aware of all these treasures or we recognized them only in theory, whereas now we live together all that we share with other Christians.

Furthermore, we experienced that with the presence of Jesus among us, fruit of the spirituality we share, such a strong bond is created among us that it makes us repeat with Saint Paul, "Who will separate us from the love of Christ?" (Rm 8:35). No one can separate us because it's Christ who binds us together.

We call this way of living the "dialogue of life." We also call it the "dialogue of the people," because we feel that we form among ourselves "one Christian people" which involves lay people, but also monks, men and women religious, deacons, priests, pastors, bishops, because the people of God includes everyone.

The "dialogue of the people" is not a grassroots dialogue that sets itself against or alongside that of the Church leaders or directors, but rather a dialogue in which all Christians can participate.

The people who live this dialogue form a leaven within the ecumenical movement. They inspire everyone to understand that since we are baptized Christians capable of loving one another, we can all contribute toward fulfilling the last prayer of Jesus for unity.

God truly gave rise to something new through the charism of unity that he gave us. Previously everyone went off on their own, but now each is interested in the others. Because of the reciprocal love that circulates among us, we come to know more about our different traditions and we appreciate the specific gifts that each one has, as well as all that we hold in common. This increases among us the "dialogue of charity." Jesus in our midst has brought us to live in communion and made us brothers and sisters to one another.

The "miracle" the world is waiting for

Commenting on a Word of Life for the month of January, in which the Week of Prayer for Christian Unity occurs, Chiara recalls the centripetal force of Jesus in the midst. United together, even though we belong to different ecclesial communities, we will be able to bear witness to God in the world.

From the commentary on the Word of Life
January 1999

"God will dwell with them, and they will be his people" (Rv 21:3).

It is therefore not so far off nor unattainable the day that will mark the fulfilment of all the promises of the Old Testament: "My dwelling place shall be with them; and I will be their God and they shall be my people" (Ez 37:27).

Everything is already fulfilled in Jesus who continues to be present, beyond his historical existence, among those who live according to the new law of mutual love, the law that constitutes them as a people, as the people of God.

This Word of Life is therefore a pressing call, especially for us Christians, a call to bear witness to the presence of God with our love. "By this everyone will know that you are my disciples, if you have love for one another" (Jn 13:35). If the new commandment of Jesus is lived in this way, it lays the foundations for the presence of Jesus among people.

We can do nothing if this presence is not assured. It is his presence that gives meaning to the divine fraternity that Jesus brought on earth for all humankind. . . .

But it is up to us, Christians, above all, even though we belong to different ecclesial communities, to show the world the marvelous spectacle of one single people, made up of every ethnic group, race and culture, of adults and children, of the sick and the healthy. A single people of which one can say, as once was said of the early Christians: "Look at how they love one another and are ready to give their lives for each other."[65]

This is the miracle that humanity is waiting for, so that it can hope once more. This is the contribution necessary for ecumenical progress in the journey towards the full and visible unity of all Christians. It is a

---

65. Tertullian, *Apologeticum* 39, 7.

"miracle" within our reach, or rather, within his reach, who, dwelling among his own united by love, can change the destiny of the world by leading the whole of humanity towards unity.

5. In the Hour of Trial

Commenting on a Word of Life, Chiara reminds us that Jesus in the midst is also consolation and assurance in the hour of trial, both for the Church as a whole, as well as for every individual Christian.

From the commentary on the Word of Life
August 1981

"Take heart, it is I; do not be afraid" (Mt 14:27).

In the moment of trial, Jesus wants the whole Church and every Christian to take courage, not to succumb. He wants them to trust in him completely, despite appearances. Above all, he wants them to live in such a way that he is always present among them. And he indicated how to do this when he said: "Where two or three are gathered in my name, I am there among them" (Mt 18:20). For when he is present, danger is far away. As soon as Jesus and Peter "got into the boat, the wind ceased" (Mt 14:32).

Let's set out to live the divine life we have been given, striving together to do all that we can so that he will never be absent from us.

To be united in his name means to be united in him, in the reality he brings, in his will, which is, above all, his commandment: "Love one another as I have loved you" (Jn 13:34).

If we do this, if we are ready to love one another as he loved us, he will be among us. And what better companion can we have in this life? He will open up for all of us the way to eternity.

Chapter VI

Jesus in the Midst
and the Renewal of the World

Permeating the Social Fabric
With the Light of God

Jesus is truly God and truly man; he "beame humanity" by assuming every dimension of human life. Therefore, those who live with Jesus in the midst, both "as individuals and together with others" are capable of bringing the new and fruitful life of God into every part of society. According to Chiara, it is impossible to renew society without God. We cannot presume to do it by ourselves, without allowing God, directly or indirectly, to work through us. This also applies to the faithful of non-Christian religions and to those who claim to be agnostics or atheists, because God has planted "the seeds of the Word" within each person, giving them the capacity to do good (see Ad Gentes, *11[66]). In this sense, we can also see the validity of Chiara's desire to form an "exterior castle," parallel to the "interior castle" of Saint Teresa of Avila (see chapter 4). In this chapter, we want to highlight the cultural and social impact of living the sentence, "where two or more. . ."*

---

66. *To the Nations,* the Second Vatican Council's decree on missionary activity.

1. Jesus in the Midst Renews All Human Experience

Christian and human activities

During an open dialogue with the readers of the Italian Focolare magazine Città Nuova, *Chiara took the opportunity offered to her by a question from one of the readers to reaffirm the social nature of the Gospel and to explain—between the lines—the communitarian nature of the spirituality of unity. The Gospel lived in this way never leaves things as they are but leads humanity towards the fulfilment of God's plan.*

Question: If Christianity were lived authentically, shouldn't it have an impact not only on the spiritual and intellectual dimensions of life, but also on all our work and everyday activities?

Yes, because by "Christian" we mean a "new person" who lives in the place where the "old person" has died, or rather, is kept dead, being alive in Christ who lives in the Christian. However, we cannot become "new" people unless we accept *everything* that Christ taught and commanded us to do.

For example, Christians who limit themselves to governing their own moral and spiritual life according to the laws of the Gospel are lacking in something if they do not help others to do the same. An individualistic Christianity is an absurdity, because it eliminates a major portion of the Gospel, above all, the parts regarding loving others *as* oneself and mutual love.

An authentic Christianity is communitarian by its very nature. This was true even for the hermits who did not live for themselves, but for the Church. The Christian life always reflects the life of the Trinity, where there are three Persons and therefore, more than just one.

If Christianity is lived in this way, if the Gospel is really lived, the "new person" is new in *everything*, being governed inwardly by the spirit of Christ who "renews the face of the earth."

If we see that Christianity does not influence enough both the intellectual and the more concrete aspects of life, we have to admit that it is not the Christian life that Christ proclaimed. After all, the new person is nothing other than "another Christ" and just as the historical Christ revolutionized his world, so "another Christ" cannot help but revolutionize the world around them.

The true world is that of Jesus in our midst

Those who live the spirituality of unity feel the desire to establish constructive and positive relationships with everyone, even with those who think very differently from them or have various political, religious, or cultural points of view. But it can happen that when others perceive that you come from the "other side of the fence," you are not well received.

From a dialogue between Chiara and the community of the Focolare in Tuscany
Florence, Italy, September 17, 2000

We are often immersed in an anti-clerical society. Even though we try to present the Ideal with terminology acceptable to everyone, barriers sometimes come up if people perceive a religious dimension to our life. This reaction is even stronger if they feel that we are involved with the Church. How can we go beyond these walls and offer the light of the charism, with all its innovative and universal significance for society?

We have to launch ourselves like the early Christians did. After we have given the witness of our life, once Christ is in our midst, let's give him the floor, allow him to speak. The early Christians spoke of the great novelty, the good news that God has come to save us. They spoke, they evangelized. By evangelizing and speaking, they brought people to God and formed communities.

That's exactly what Saint Paul did. He made people come alive, he loved them, they loved each other, he spoke, but the others also spoke, he formed communities. What did these communities do? They created a different kind of world, one necessary for us Christians, because Jesus said: "You are in the world, but not of the world" (see Jn 17:16). So where can we go? Up on a mountain, all on our own? Up in the clouds? Where can we go? We need a world also for ourselves, here and now, because we are in the midst of the world. And so the Gospel and the Christian revolution created this new world for us; it is also being created by our Movement. . . . Jesus in our midst creates our environment, our world, and we have to know that *this* is our world and not that other one. We should not belong to the other world, we cannot be part of that world, we have to be immersed in *this* world.

When something from that world disturbs us, like temptations against purity or certain ideas, etc., we have to run back to *our* world. That's where we will feel once more the power of our faith, we will be strengthened and feel again the ardor to move forward and to spread this world of ours more and more. In this way, little by little, we will change the world.

So, we should never be intimidated by anything or anyone. People often tell me: "But Chiara, we are in India, there are millions of people here, how can we manage? We only have two small focolare houses, one in Bombay. . . . What can we possibly do?" To begin with, Jesus didn't worry about how many people were in the Roman Empire! And not even in the Holy Land before starting; he just started! Statistics are our ruin, they discourage us; we always have to be "up." If there are two of us with Jesus in our midst, we possess the whole world, because we have Christ; we have the one who has conquered the world.

What we need is the light of Jesus, his wisdom

Witnesses are needed, especially for those who make a spiritual and moral commitment to live the Gospel. People who give witness inspire us to fulfil God's plan for us. Chiara Lubich has been, and continues to be, a witness and a model for thousands of people who want to bring God into the world. Hence the very personal tone of the answer that follows.

To a congress of the women focolarine
Castel Gandolfo, Italy, December 30, 2002

More and more we see the explosion of the light of your charism that regenerates and illuminates every aspect of human life. We want to follow you with the same passion that you have. What do you expect from us so that we can keep up with you?

To keep in step with my soul I expect many things of you, all that I expect of myself, too, of course. First of all, that you take as your own—and don't wait until afterwards, when I am not here anymore—take as your own the legacy I am leaving you, that is, the possibility of having Jesus in our midst, of allowing him to return on earth, to be re-born.

I expect you to make this legacy your own immediately, never to deviate from it, never to waste it. Rather—like the precious pearl—you should sell everything to have this treasure, because he is the one who guides us in life, his light is what we need, not the light of human reasoning or of scholarly knowledge. We need *his* light, the light of Jesus; we need *his* wisdom.

Keep Jesus in the midst and do whatever you want

From the perspective of how people live out the charism within the Focolare Movement, we see that there are two distinct vocations, based, however, on the same commitment to give oneself wholeheartedly to God. Some people feel the call to make a choice of God in which they concretely leave father, mother, children, fields, etc., and in this way aim to "bring God into the world." Others feel the call to "remain" in their own environment, maintaining all the natural and social ties that this entails, but with a free and total commitment to "bring the world to God." Those who live this second vocation within the Movement are called the "volunteers of God." The following reply is addressed to one of them.

June 13, 1987

Listening to the answers you gave in March last year to those responsible for the focolare houses, we feel that they are relevant for us, too. Is there anything in particular that you could add for us who are responsible for the unity among the volunteers?

I don't feel there is anything special to add! We have the General Statutes for everyone, and then we have the specific regulations for the volunteers. In the Statutes that apply to everyone, it says that the "rule of rules" is Jesus in the midst, that we first have to have Jesus in our midst and then we can work in politics. . . . We can do many things.

I am certain that Jesus in the midst of the focolarini has a particular tint because that Jesus in the midst illuminates the vocation of the focolare. Jesus in the midst of the volunteers has another expression, another tint, another beauty, because it enlightens people who are volunteers, but we all have to do the same thing, the same thing is the basis of everything for all of us.

Saint Augustine said: "Love and do whatever you want." I would say to those in our Movement: "Keep Jesus in the midst and do whatever you want!" In the sense that you will bring about a new way of doing politics, a new way of doing economics and a new way of expressing moral issues.

Do whatever you want, as long as you have Jesus in the midst. I will close my eyes and tell the whole Movement to close their eyes to what you are doing, because I am certain that with Jesus in the midst you will do everything perfectly well. With Jesus in the midst you will do wonderful things.

I say this because you will talk things over among yourselves, and you will immediately understand what to do. You will give birth to as many things as possible, because there is such urgent need right now. It is a bit like the Incarnation. The coming of Jesus was awaited for many centuries, and then he became incarnate in the Virgin Mary. . . . People longed for him for many centuries! At this moment, we feel a little like those people that longed for him for centuries. . . . We long for a new humanity to explode *now*, and for it to explode we have to have Jesus in the midst, because for it to explode we need beautiful nuclei, because then everything can explode! But let's really keep Jesus in our midst and then do what we want! It will all be good!

And don't slow down. Some of you have a special interest in the adoption of children, others have a special interest in working with the disabled, others who have a special interest in . . . But they are not "special interests," they are "gifts," as Saint Paul says: "Each person has spiritual gifts, special graces that are given to them by the Holy Spirit for the common good" (see 1 Cor 12:4-11).

It is these small graces that we see in our volunteers, who sometimes write to me saying that their activity is not understood, that people say . . . "Oh, he is so involved with his business, he has that little project, he . . ." Instead, we could start exactly from there to develop bigger projects in the New Humanity Movement. So there is no difference among us. Of course, the beautiful fruits that result from what you do are different, but the spirituality is the same and there is only one Jesus!

The family reflects the life of the Trinity

The life of the family has undoubtedly been enlightened and revitalized by the presence of Jesus in the midst of family members. Chiara spoke about this often. Here we propose a passage from her talk given on the occasion of her honorary doctorate in theology, awarded by the University of Trnava in Slovakia.

Castel Gandolfo, Italy, June 23, 2003

The life of the family is inseparably intertwined with the mystery of the life of God himself, which is unity and Trinity. Genesis tells us (see Gn 1: 27-28) that when God created humankind in his image, he created us as man and woman, and placed the human person at the apex of creation. As we read in *Mulieris Dignitatem*,[67] in the beginning, God formed a family, made of a man and a woman called to live a communion of love that would reflect in the world the communion of love that exists in God.

Thus, "in the light of the New Testament," as John Paul II states, "it is possible to envision the original model of the family in God himself, as Trinity, as a communion of persons . . ."

In the spirituality of unity, we go to God by loving others, especially those closest to us. Therefore, the evangelical love of husband and wife, their love for the children, and the mutual love among them all makes the members of the family experience the presence of Jesus in their midst. In this way, they reflect the love that is within the Trinity.

---

67. *On the Dignity of Women*, apostolic letter by Pope John Paul II, Rome, 1988.

In spite of the fact that families today are continuously under attack, it is my conviction, based on experience, that the spirituality of unity can give a valid contribution to the fulfilment of the family according to God's plan for it.

2. "Peace I Leave With You; My Peace I Give to You" (Jn 14:27)

To be instruments of peace and brotherhood

When people have Jesus present among them, they experience peace, which is a fundamental human value and is also the basis for good social and political relationships. Ambrogio Lorenzetti expressed this reality very well in his famous allegorical paintings on "Good and Bad Government."[68] *Chiara speaks repeatedly of peace as the main goal of interreligious and political dialogue. The passage quoted here illustrates this very well.*

To the Assembly of the World Conference of Religions for Peace
Amman, Jordan, November 29, 1999

Clearly, anyone who aspires to remove the mountains of hatred and violence faces a daunting task. But—and this is important—what is impossible for millions of separate, isolated individuals becomes possible when people make reciprocal love, mutual understanding and unity the motivating force of their lives.

---

68. Cycle of frescoes preserved in the Palazzo Pubblico of Siena, Italy

To achieve all of this, we know that there is a motive, a key, a name. When we of different religions enter into dialogue, that is, when we are open to one another in a dialogue based on mutual kindness, reciprocal esteem and respect, we also open ourselves up to God. In the words of John Paul II, "we allow God to be present in our midst."[69]

This is the great fruit of our mutual love and is the hidden force that gives vigor and success to our work for peace. The Gospel announces to Christians that if two or more are united in genuine love, Christ himself, who is Peace, is present among them and therefore, in each one of them. And what greater guarantee than the presence of God, what greater opportunity can there be for those who want to be instruments of brotherhood and peace?

We can overcome prejudice with him

Considering human society without reference to God and the unfolding of history often produce obstacles to the path of peace and the "civilization of love." Jesus came to overcome the world in this sense also.

From a page of her diary
November 7, 1968

I will try to understand, we will try to understand together how to make the light of Jesus have a greater impact on our ultramodern world, which is, however, thwarted by so much prejudice, as for example, racial

---

69. John Paul II, Discourse to non-Christian representatives in Madras, India, 5 February 1986, *Osservatore Romano* (Weekly English Edition) 10 February 1986:14.

discrimination, which makes it regress, even in a country that is a world leader.

One thing is certain, and Jesus in the midst will keep repeating this: there is neither Greek nor Jew . . . neither black nor white. We are all one in Christ Jesus.

He is the author of peace

From a page of her diary
February 7, 1981

So, let's get to work! Let's keep perfect unity with everyone, certainly without any rifts, but not even a little tarnished. In short, let's be everywhere and always peacemakers, first of all in our dealings with God and then with all our neighbors. And like Mary, by bringing the presence of Jesus in our midst, we bring the author of peace himself.

3. A Healthy Social Body
in All its Components

The local action cells,[70] a basis for regenerating the social fabric

With this innovative idea, Chiara responds to the need that people feel to bring Jesus into their professional and social environments. It is a program particularly

---

70. Local action cells are made up of two or more people in the same work environment who want to bring more unity and brotherly love there by keeping Jesus present among them.

suited to lay people, indeed it is their characteristic "skill," and makes them specialists in promoting the "health of the social body." In ecclesial terms, Chiara goes so far as to use an expression that is quite audacious: "Jesus in the midst is the sacrament of the laity."

From an answer to the school for the volunteers of God
Loppiano, Italy, May 5, 1989

The local action cells are the "focolares" of society. What relationship should the members have with one another? Should there be only work or also communion of soul? And to what extent?

When the members of a local action cell do not meet on a daily basis, as for example, town councilors, but only periodically and often with many different kinds of problems to resolve, how can we guarantee the presence of Jesus in the midst so that it can be a true focolare of society?

In the meetings of the local action cells, what role do the focolarini have? Should they be present?

This reality of the local action cells is very, very important. We have spread the Movement in many parts of society, among many people, beginning with the base, beginning with the people, as Jesus did. He didn't go around looking for the leaders. There were a few, but for the most part, he began with the ordinary people.

Now, however, we are reaching a rather high level. There are people in the Parliament who were once Gen 3[71], and are now adults and members of Parliament. In

---

71. Gen 3 are children from the ages of 9 to 17, representing the third generation of the Focolare Movement. They are formed in the spirituality of unity and make a commitment to live it in their daily activities.

the different environments—in the schools, factories and shops, everywhere, and in parliaments, too—we can find two, three, four persons who belong to our Movement. And so we told them: "Get together, love one another as we should, establish the presence of Jesus and see how you can transform that environment into something with good values, into a Christian environment. Try to see how you can spread love to the others and how you can change the structures or create new ones."

Naturally, these people who make up the local action cells have already been cultivated in their branches, in the different movements within our Movement, so they don't have to spend time discussing the spirituality, or to share what they have in their souls. They should deal with concrete matters, for example, discussing what to do with regard to a particular law, asking each other: "What steps should we take so that it passes, or so that it doesn't pass, etc., etc." Or: "There is something new in this school, we have to see if it is good to promote it." Or: "There is a proposal to open new schools, but is it the case or not?" So they should get down to work immediately, because they already receive their spiritual formation in their own branch or movement.

Then there are the focolarini who make sure that the "fire" is burning. So with these two supports, there is no need to spend time. . . . We should meet and be ready at once to have Jesus in the midst, because he promised his presence wherever there are two or more united in his name.

I have the impression that these local action cells are of enormous importance, because if we do not enter into society, into humanity, etc., our Movement will remain too spiritual, and God does not want this.

Jesus became incarnate. He became a man. So at a certain point, the spirituality has to give rise to a new humanity, a new society. Only in this way can we hope to achieve such great goals, as I said before, like the unity of peoples, etc.

So even those who are town councilors, who meet occasionally, have to come to the meeting ready to have unity with one another, to clear up their differences at once, to get down to the business at hand, to say: "Look, that particular place would be open to the spirit of unity. Let's try to speak with the director, with the principal. . . . See, there's the possibility of establishing another local action cell there, in that office, maybe between. . . Or in that school between the janitor and the principal, or between the janitor, the teacher and the principal." So they keep Jesus in their midst and Jesus enters.

I have the impression that in this era, through us lay people, Jesus wants to come out of the tabernacles. He wants to go out in the midst of the world. He wants to live in our midst. Indeed, Jesus in the midst, I don't know if I am wrong—the priests can tell me—in my opinion, Jesus in the midst is the sacrament of the laity.

Find the right words that everyone understands

However, it is necessary to use the right words in the right place. This is how Chiara answers a question relating to a very specific cultural context in Great Britain.

London, England, November 16, 1996

One of the aspects of English culture is the fear of submitting to something collective. Some expressions like "make unity," "cutting off one's head," "unity or death,"[72] which we often use, make people feel very uncomfortable. Are these phrases an essential part of the Ideal or can these concepts be adapted to the local culture to better convey their meaning?

We certainly don't ask anyone to subject themselves to collectivism—absolutely not! We ask that all together we build the community, unity, and this is the will of God, because we have to live according to the lifestyle of the Trinity, which is a community of three persons in one.

With regard to the words we use, here again, it's a question of enculturation. We should not use words that others don't understand or misunderstand. We have to use the right words. So, instead of saying, "Make yourselves one," it's enough to say, "Love." Loving is making ourselves one. Instead of saying, "We have to cut off our heads," we should say, "We have to love to the point of being ready to give our life, and therefore, to put aside our thoughts in order to penetrate those of others, in order to understand the other person." "Either unity or death" isn't something we should say to others. . . . First of all, it's not a word of God. "Either unity or death" is a motto of the focolarini. It's enough to tell others, "You know, unity is a strong commitment; it's not something to be taken lightly . . . or of little account. It's really something strong." Do you understand what I mean?

---

72. These are strong expressions used by Chiara in the early years of the Movement, to mean that we need to be totally empty in front of others to receive what they say ("make unity"), die to ourselves and all our own ideas to be at one with others ("cut off your head, remove your ideas") or choosing unity above all else ("unity or death").

So you should change the words. When you go to another country, you learn a whole new language, all the more should you change these words in order to . . . enculturate yourselves.

4. A New Light for All Areas of Knowledge

The peole of unity offer a new doctrine

Chiara was always fascinated by the Truth with a capital "T," that is, God. And she always felt an overwhelming desire to find the Truth in every area of human knowledge. Whenever Truth is overshadowed, incomplete, or even sterile, it should be revitalized and made visible to everyone through the presence of Jesus in us and among us. This can be done through "good practice" that should be implemented by every upright professional. Speaking to a group of people of the Focolare Movement who are committed to politics at various levels, Chiara reiterated this fundamental point of her experience and her thought.

Excerpts from a talk to members of the Movement of Politics and Policy for Unity
Castel Gandolfo, Italy, June 9, 2000

Since the early days of our Movement, we have always been aware that the charism of unity brings its own culture, a culture that is the fruit of Christian tradition, but at the same time is a new culture, because of the light of the charism. However, it has been the growth in number of the people of unity and the spreading of our Ideal outside the structures of the

Focolare Movement, that has highlighted the specific characteristic of this culture, and led to the study of its doctrine, not only in the field of theology, but also in philosophy, politics, economics, psychology, art, etc. This is what has been done for the past ten years by the group we call the "Abba School," in which experts from different disciplines work together with me.

This encounter between the "people of unity" and the doctrine underlying their life has recently brought about what we call the "inundations." It is a term suggested to us by Saint John Chrysostom (who spoke of "rivers of living water" inundating the world). Authentic new movements have developed, in particular in the field of economics, with the project of the Economy of Communion, and in politics, with the Movement of Politics and Policy for Unity (MppU) which promotes a new political culture.

This new vision of politics does not give rise to a new party. Instead, it changes the method of engaging in politics. While each one remains faithful to their own genuine political ideals, the politician of unity loves everyone, and therefore, in every circumstance, seeks for what unites.

We would like to envision politics—as we mentioned earlier—perhaps as it has never been conceived of before. We would like to give birth—I venture to say—to a "politics of Jesus," embodying what he wants and what he can do through us, wherever we are. Thus people might be involved in national and regional governments, in city councils, in political parties, in various civic and political committees, representing different points of view. Unity, lived among us in this way, should then be brought, like leaven, into the individual parties, among parties, within institutions, into every area of public life, and in relations among countries.

Every people will then be able to go beyond its own borders and look outwards, loving the country of the others as their own, so that the presence of Jesus can also be established among nations, and make humanity one universal family. This goes beyond the limited concept of an international society, because the relationships among individuals, groups and nations will facilitate breaking down divisions and barriers of all kinds.

This is the objective of the MppU, which is beginning to flourish today in different parts of the world and has shown itself capable of creating new projects and attracting people from every level and of every political persuasion. The MppU includes members of the Focolare Movement who are involved in politics in some way, either as a profession or in the effort to carry out their civic duty, and they are joined by many other people who have come to know and live the Ideal of unity, even though they do not specifically belong to the Movement as such.

Who better than Jesus can tell us about God?

Among the various areas of knowledge, the first one to focus on is theology. We begin this section with a question that comes from a young person during an ecumenical meeting in which Chiara had explained the most important points of the spirituality of unity as a very fruitful way of recomposing unity among the Churches.

An answer to a meeting at the Ecumenical Institute of Bossey
Bossey, Switzerland, October 26, 2002

> *My name is Karen Jobson from England. I'm in the graduate school here in Bossey. I was really moved by what you said, and I thank you for it. I can see that your whole life is based on your spirituality. My question is very simple: Are the theologians wasting their time?*

No, they are not. This spirituality is also an opportunity for theologians. We have a group formed by about thirty theologians, philosophers, scientists, doctors, politicians, etc. Our basic rule is that of always having Christ in our midst. Therefore, before beginning any of our meetings, we declare to each other that we are ready to die for one another, to die to ourselves so that we can listen to the other person, so that we can enter into the mentality of the others, to the point of having the same idea, just one thought.

Paul wanted us Christians to be of one mind, which is the mind of Christ, of Christ in our midst. It might not be mine, or yours, but it is Jesus'. Therefore, it is for theologians, too. If they make this spirituality their own and live it wholeheartedly—something superficial is not enough, one has to know the spirituality, live it, apply it—they will have an enormous advantage because they will have the theologian *par excellence* among them, the exegete *par excellence*, the philosopher *par excellence*. They will have *everything* in their midst, because Jesus himself will be in their midst, and he will suggest things to them. There *is* hope for the theologians. They aren't wasting time. There is hope. In the meantime, they do what they can.

Forming the person-in-relationship

In the passages that follow, which conclude this chapter, we offer a substantial overview of Chiara's thought expressed in her lectures given on the occasions of the numerous honorary doctorates she received from various universities throughout the world. We take as an example the doctorates in pedagogy and psychology since these two disciplines are particularly dedicated to the human person. Here we can see that the powerful light of truth, which comes from Jesus present among people united in his name, has an impact that goes far beyond the religious and spiritual sphere.

Excerpts from a lecture on education given at the Catholic University of America
Washington, DC, November 10, 2000

In our approach to education, in which the spiritual and human aspects of life penetrate one another and become one (because of the Incarnation), this utopia is not a dream, nor an illusion, nor an unattainable goal. It is already present here among us, and we see its fruits when we live out Jesus' words: "Where two or three are gathered in my name, I am there among them" (Mt 18:20). In this way, education's goal, its highest aim, becomes a reality.

Thus we experience the fullness of God's life, which Jesus has given us, in a relationship modelled on the Trinity. This is the most genuine form of social relationships, in which a wonderful synthesis is achieved between the two goals of education: to teach the individual and to build up the community. We believe that our experience of living a communitarian spirituality, modelled on the Trinity, brings to fulfilment many ideas held by outstanding men and women throughout the history of education. Their initial premises were often different from ours, but they insisted on the importance of education to build up a society founded on authentic democratic relationships. One example among many would be the great contribution offered by John Dewey to education throughout the world, beginning with the United States. We also find many similarities in the recent concept of "service-learning," which affirms that the formation of a person should also involve formation in and for the community.

Of course, our experience of community life is based on Jesus' invitation: "Love one another as I have loved you. . . That they may all be one" (see Jn 15:12; 17:21). This motivation is religious in nature, but it has extraordinary effects in the field of education.

The goal that has always been assigned to education (to "form the human person, so as to render him or her independent") is implemented, almost paradoxically, by forming the person-in-relationship. For us, this means forming the human person in the image of the Trinity, one who is capable of continually transcending self in the context of keeping Jesus present in our midst. All the members of the Movement follow this spiritual and educational practice of mutual love, to the point of becoming completely one with others. In fact, all are called to live a communitarian experience in small groups and in this way work towards the achievement of the greatest of all goals, expressed in Jesus' last prayer: "That they may all be one." As instruments under his guidance, we want to spend our lives for the fulfilment of this goal, which is a utopia and yet a reality.

It is through this educational process that we as individuals and as community become capable of meeting one another, entering into a dialogue and working together with other persons, other Movements, etc. And it is also through this comprehensive educational process that, with God's grace, we can aspire to reach our personal and communal sanctity.[73]

Everyone needs to be affirmed so as to be gift for others

In the following text, there is no explicit reference to the verse of Matthew 18:20. But it is implied, in particular when Chiara describes the nature of the Christian community.

Excerpts from an address upon reception of an honorary doctorate in psychology
University of Malta, February 26, 1999

Psychologically speaking, it is impossible for an individual to have a sense of personal identity unless there are other people who recognize them as a person.

Psychologists of all schools agree that human beings need to affirm one another in their individuality by means of genuine relationships and interaction.

In fact, it is necessary to feel and be recognized as distinct and unique, in order to be a gift of self for other people.

However, in order to be a personal gift it is necessary to enter into communion with others.

---

73. Lubich, *Essential Writings*, 219-224.

And herein lies the difference between so-called interest groups and the Christian community as Jesus intended. An interest group is made up of individuals who come together with a particular goal in mind (athletic clubs, civic, political or religious associations, trade unions, schools, study groups, etc.) and whose interaction is limited to carrying out those common interests. As for anything outside the realm of these common interests, these individuals remain closed in their own world.

The Christian community, instead, is not formed for extrinsic reasons, but because it is in the very character of love to create communion.

Experience confirms that this type of community is possible. It is clear that the motivation to bring about such a community comes from Jesus' invitation: "Love one another as I have loved you . . . that they may all be one" (see Jn 15:12; 17:21). Obviously this is religious in nature. But the psychological effects are extraordinary because each individual, being in a relationship of love with others, is, as a consequence, fulfilled as an authentic person.[74]

---

74. Ibid., 225-29.

Epilogue

As a conclusion, we include here some passages from the address of Pope Francis during his visit to the little town of Loppiano on May 10, 2018. In his address we can understand how much the reality of Jesus in the midst, which he recognizes in the life of Loppiano, is in tune with the direction in which the Holy Spirit is leading the Church and humanity today.

Even though the Pope did not quote Matthew 18:20, and did not speak explicitly of Jesus in the midst, it is not difficult to recognize the same concept described in this book in what he calls the spirituality of "the we." And at the end he invites all present to place themselves "at the school of Mary, to learn how to know Jesus, how to live with him, (at the school) of Jesus present in each one of us and in our midst."

The charism of unity is a providential stimulus and a powerful support for experiencing the evangelical mystic of "the we," that is, walking together in the history of the people of our time as "one heart and soul" (see Acts 4:32), discovering and loving concretely as "members of one another" (see Rom 12:5). Jesus prayed to the Father for this: "that they may all be one as you and I are one" (see Jn 17: 21). He himself showed us the way, right up to the complete gift of all in his unfathomable emptying of self on the cross (see Mk 15:34; Phil 2:6-8). . . . This is the spirituality of "the we" that you have to bring ahead and that saves us from all selfishness and every egotistical desire. The spirituality of "the we."

It is not only a spiritual fact. If we live it and authentically and courageously carry out its various dimensions, it is also a concrete reality with formidable results on the social, cultural, political, economic levels. . . . Jesus redeemed not only the individual person, but also social relationships (see *Evangelii Gaudium*, n. 178). Taking this fact seriously means giving a new countenance to the "city of men" according to God's plan of love. . . .

In Loppiano, you live the experience of journeying together, according to the style of a synod, as the people of God. This is the firm and indispensable foundation underlying everything here: the school of the people of God, in which the one who teaches and leads is the one Master (see Mt 23:10), and where the dynamic is that of mutual listening and the exchange of gifts among all. . . .

The often dramatic needs that challenge us from all sides cannot leave us in peace, but rather demand the maximum from us, always trusting in the grace of God.

In the epochal change that we are experiencing—it is not an epoch of change but a change of epoch—it is important to be committed not only to the encounter among people, cultures and peoples and to a coalition among civilizations. We also need to be committed to overcoming together the epochal challenge of building a shared culture of encounter and a global civilization of coalition. . . .

How can we know and follow the Holy Spirit? By practicing collective discernment. That is, by gathering in assembly around the risen Jesus, the Lord and Master, to hear what the Holy Spirit is telling us today as a Christian community (see Rv 2:7) and to discover together, in this atmosphere, the call to live the Gospel that God helps us to hear within the historical situation in which we live.[75]

---

75. Talk given by Pope Francis during the meeting with the Focolare Movement at the sanctuary of "Mary the Theotokos," in Loppiano on May 10, 2018.

New City Press

New City Press is one of more than 20 publishing houses sponsored by the Focolare, a movement founded by Chiara Lubich to help bring about the realization of Jesus' prayer: "That all may be one" (John 17:21). In view of that goal, New City Press publishes books and resources that enrich the lives of people and help all to strive toward the unity of the entire human family. We are a member of the Association of Catholic Publishers.

www.newcitypress.com
202 Comforter Blvd.
Hyde Park, New York

Periodicals
Living City Magazine
www.livingcitymagazine.com

Join our mailing list for discounts and promotions
at www.newcitypress.com